Brain Health

AND

Wellness

Brain Health
AND
Wellness

Dr. Paul Nussbaum

Word Association Publishers
205 Fifth Avenue
Tarentum, Pennsylvania 15084

ISBN: 1-932205-64-0
Library of Congress Control Number: 2003110783

Word Association Publishers
205 Fifth Avenue
Tarentum, Pennsylvania 15084
www.wordassociation.com

Paul David Nussbaum, Ph.D.
Clinical Neuropsychologist
ageon@zoominternet.net
www.paulnussbaum.com

Table of Contents

To Paul David II

Preface
Why it Matters

As a child I would often hear my mother's demand to "respect your elders." Perhaps more than any other, this message directed my career towards the older American. As a young man in my early twenties, I recall applying for a part-time position in a new nursing home near my hometown Pittsburgh. Fortunately, there was a kind administrator who actually created a position for me with the title "research assistant." She explained to me that the nursing home had just opened a new Alzheimer's unit and my task was to determine if a group activity for the residents had any measurable benefit. As it turned out, a psychologist named Larry Haddad and I completed a small study that demonstrated some benefit in mood for those residents suffering Alzheimer's disease who engaged in a daily group activity. The paper was presented at a scientific meeting and my career in gerontology had begun. Dr. Haddad remains a strong friend and colleague twenty years later.

Actually, my path towards older adults began much earlier. I recall visits to my maternal grandparents, two Italians with all of the typical and wonderful tradition of their nationality. My grandmother was a tough lady who always seemed to have enough food to feed between ten to fifteen people. This was true at any time of the day. She would take hold of my hand and lead me to the basement where she would demonstrate her skill in preparing pasta from scratch. My grandfather was no less impressive. He was a man who immigrated with his wife to

America without a job or much money. He secured employment in the railroad industry, raised nine children, and put most of them through college. Indeed, of the nine children, two became teachers, three became nurses, one a priest, and one a surgeon. The other two children focused their attention on the home where much work was done to maintain a busy household. Grandfather would sit in his chair, smoke a cigar and drink red wine. He had the biggest garden I had ever seen and the foods he produced were used in the wonderful meals prepared by my grandmother.

From these two impressive people in my early life, I learned the importance of the meal, the family, hard work, discipline, and that older people have much to teach. My grandparents were in their late seventies and eighties when I knew them, hardly the age when most believe such productivity is possible. I learned early that productivity and functionality have little to do with chronological age, a lesson that has served me well in life. Unfortunately, I never met my paternal grandparents. I know they were German and produced four children, all of who are alive and successful today. My mother was the youngest in her family, my father the oldest in his. They are nearing their eighties and remain highly involved in life. Indeed, my father continues to work as a salesman and actually has been hired by several different companies in the past decade. There is no harder worker than my mother, nor any greater disciplinarian. Clearly, my grandmother lives through my mother.

The personal lessons I learned in childhood shaped my attitude and approach to life and certainly towards my work with older persons. For the past 17 years I have done little more than work with older adults. In that time, I have learned much about the human condition, about family, about grief, and about disease. More importantly, I have learned about perseverance and the greatness of the human spirit, especially when confronted with tremendous adversity.

x

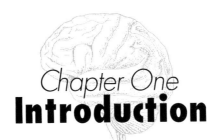

Chapter One
Introduction

Martha was an older woman sitting alone in a chair crying and in despair. The nursing home where she resided was filled with activity and noise. I asked her why she was crying and she informed me that her children needed their dinner and she did not know how to get to them. Martha had an accurate memory for she once had prepared the meals for her children. Unfortunately, her memory was out of context. She was unaware of the fact that she was living in a nursing home, and more importantly, that her children were now on their own preparing their own meals.

Harold was an older man who frequently wandered, sometimes out of the nursing home where he lived. This placed him and the entire organization at risk for his safety. The administrator had asked me if I could do something to keep Harold in the facility. I was afraid of this situation because a person who wanders may have a specific plan or motive that is empowered by an inner intensity difficult to modify. One day I ran to Harold as he was walking away in the parking lot. There I asked him where he was going to which he responded, "I need to go begin farming." As with Martha, Harold reported an accurate memory (he was a farmer) that was out of context. My remedy for the situation was to inform Harold that the garden was in the back of the building (we had an enclosed area there) and we needed him to lead the farming there. He became interested and joined me in returning to the nursing home. Harold nurtured the garden, growing tomatoes and other vegetables that were used in the meals of residents at the facility. Placing his accurate memory in an accurate context had reduced his wandering.

Martha and Harold suffered Alzheimer's Disease (AD), a progressive dementia that invades the brain and slowly erases the person's memory and with it their life story. Alzheimer's represents the "poster child" for human brain disease! The tragedy of this disease is multifactorial with significant distress experienced by the person afflicted and the family caregivers. Over the years, so many families have called me to learn about the disease and to express their grief. For any child or other family caregiver, there is no formula for how to cope with a mother or father losing their memory and identity. Perhaps the cruelest reality of all is the fact that eventually the disease erodes the victim's memory of their family. How does one cope with their mother or father not recognizing them anymore? My experience is that this cruelty is confronted with love and compassion.

Richard was a gentleman in his seventies who would arrive at my office occasionally to express his deep feelings regarding the loss of his wife to AD. He informed me that his wife of greater than fifty years was residing in the nursing home where I had worked until May of 2001. His story was particularly emotional and his pain was expressed on each visit to me. I had a difficult time as Richard pleaded with me to do something to bring his wife back to him. He often attended my workshops on AD where I would convey some of the latest research on AD and my hopes for a cure someday. Richard used this information to seek help for his wife. Unfortunately, our progress on this disease is not at a point yet to intervene with a cure. This information was difficult to relate to Richard and more difficult for him to accept. I have met so many spouses and children who serve as the primary caregivers for their loved ones suffering AD. Their commitment and devotion to their family members has been inspiring and humbling. One cannot be exposed to these experiences and emerge unchanged. I have remained professional, but with a quiet revolt inside; I believe we must engage in an unprecedented battle to defeat this disease. I continuously search for better ways to prevent the disease, rather than rely on reacting to the disease once it has already begun its destructive course. From this foundation, I have moved conceptually to learn more about prevention and health promoting behaviors that might reduce our risk of getting AD and other diseases of the brain.

Dare to Think Different

The fact that dementia (loss of intelligence and memory) manifests clinically late in life does not necessarily mean the fundamental pathological changes underlying dementia also begin in our later years. Indeed, clinical manifestation of dementia may represent the final stage of a lifelong process of disease and dementia may actually begin in our early years of development. At this point in time, research suggests that AD begins to invade the human brain long before clinical manifestation occurs (Reiman et al., 1998). Indeed, cognitively intact individuals in late middle age (50-65 years of age) who have a genetic predisposition to AD, demonstrate reduced glucose metabolism in the precise brain regions most vulnerable to AD (Reiman et al., 1996). Similarly, magnetic resonance imaging (MRI) technology found smaller hippocampal (brain region for memory invaded by AD) volume in cognitively normal persons between the ages of 50-62 who were genetically vulnerable for AD compared to controls (Reiman et al., 1998).

Development of AD in early life has fundamental significance regarding how we approach disease prevention and more precisely health promotion. Presently, our approach of assessing AD, identifying disease, and intervening occurs late in life well after the pathological markers have begun to manifest clinically. This approach has resulted in little if any success in stopping or slowing the numbers of people affected by the disease. It would appear that our nation needs to develop a much more proactive battle against dementia with interventions beginning at the earliest years of development!

There are approximately four million Americans who suffer AD, others who suffer related dementias and these numbers are expected to rise dramatically in the next thirty to fifty years (La Rue, 1992). If a new approach to AD and related dementias is not adopted, the country will most likely experience a tremendous economic crisis and burden that our currently outdated long term care system cannot manage. Further, the family unit will experience continued economic and emotional burden, as more persons will be confronted with the inability to care for a parent who is completely dependent.

That the brain of a human genetically predisposed to AD begins to demonstrate neurophysiological change in the form of reduced glucose metabolism is both frightening and opportunistic. Clearly, the idea that a disease as cruel and devastating as AD can invade our central nervous system so early in life is worthy of anxiety. At the same time, our understanding that AD begins its damage early in life mandates we change our outdated, reactive approach to a more proactive lifestyle concept. Taken to the extreme, AD viewed as originating in childhood and causing slow but sustained damage across the lifespan necessitates an equally sustained, proactive and lifelong lifestyle that begins at the earliest of ages.

This book positions health promotion and brain wellness as a proactive approach to limit the incidence of AD and related dementias and, or to delay the onset of such neurodegenerative diseases. Intellectual reserve theory (Albert, 1995; Mortimer, 1997) (described later) provides a framework to conceptualize a healthy lifestyle for the human brain, not unlike that promoted for the heart.

Lifestyle for the Human Brain

Alzheimer's disease is a major problem that robs vibrant individuals of their life story. However, AD is not the only condition that destroys brain cells. Strokes, Parkinson's disease and many other conditions destroy brain tissue and invade vital centers of thought and behavior. This book is written as one small step towards a conceptually broader attack against neurodegenerative diseases late in life. It champions the idea that we have more control in fighting off such disease than perhaps we know. Using empirical research findings from the animal model on brain research, the book looks critically to the human being for ways to grow and maintain healthy brains across the lifespan. Much as our nation has rallied to fight off heart disease, the time has come to allocate similar attention to health promotion of the brain! Most importantly, the book is written to reflect my desire to respond to so many who have lost so much. We must awaken to a new, broader offensive on diseases of the brain not only to fight off different conditions, but also to preserve the life stories of all.

Lifestyle and health promoting behaviors starting early in life and continuing across the lifespan represent one tool in this offensive. While we may live to see the day when a "magic bullet" is created to inoculate our brains from neurodegenerative diseases, our present reality is that the bullet does not exist. In the meantime, let us all focus on prevention and health promotion for the greatest system in our body and on the planet earth—the human brain!

Promising Questions

What if our brains had *unlimited* capacity to grow, to develop, and to master multiple domains of knowledge and skill? What if we had a significant role in this process by choosing specific environmental input to our brains that fostered neuronal development? What if the qualitative and quantitative brain development *early in life* served as a predictor for vulnerability to neurodegenerative diseases late in life? What if our brains possessed the ability to *regenerate neurons*, reverse disease, and prevent destructive processes? What if our society developed and promoted *practical* approaches and programs from our new understanding of the human brain in order to encourage such neuronal development? What if our nation prioritized *brain health and wellness* with the same enthusiasm and urgency that cardiac health has received? Our dance with the "Tin Man" who found his heart would turn gracefully to a "waltz with the Scarecrow" who searched for a brain!

These are the fascinating questions that fueled the writing of this book. The idea that our brains do not have the same regenerative capacity as the rat (see Diamond, Krechi & Rosenzweig 1964) and that our brains have but one critical window of developmental opportunity early in life (see Kotulak, 1997) seems implausible. The simple observation of new skill acquisition across the lifespan raises a direct challenge to such myopic thought and thereby may require a new paradigm for lifespan neuronal development in the human. This book considers such fundamental questions and apparent paradoxes curious and perhaps ludicrous.

Relying on animal and human research, new ideas for brain development and potential are presented. Much of what we learn to be beneficial for human beings comes from research on animals. In particular, research on monkeys and other non human primates offers potentially significant insight to the possibilities for humans as there are significant similarities between the two. It is from this research that health promotion of the human brain early in life becomes paramount and deserving of unprecedented attention. This book concludes first that our brains are highly malleable and dynamic systems, which when positioned within a persistently challenging and stimulating environment, develop across the entire lifespan no less than the rat brain (explained below)! Second, this book concludes that every person maintains a critically important role in his or her brain development, that this role is life-long, and that our nation can prioritize (and financially incentivize) the encouragement of our role in order to promote health and enhancement of the human condition.

In many ways, the central nervous system of the human being represents the final frontier for discovery and understanding of our potential and our limitation. With the 1990's "Decade of the Brain" having fueled a growing momentum in brain science, society is more prepared and willing to explore the miracle that is the human brain. Our advances in neuroimaging technology have enabled an unprecedented observation of the structure and function of the billions of neurons that help to make us who we are.

The enormous amount of brain research in the past decade has generated direct challenges to long held beliefs regarding the capacity and limitations of the human brain (Gross, 2000; Van Pragg, Kempermann, & Gage, 2000). Consumers now have access to published textbooks that review findings from animal brain research (Diamond & Hopson, 1998) and articulate the potential application from the animal model to the human being (Kotulak, 1997; Snowdon, 2001; Whalley, 2001). These efforts within the current era of neuroscience render the scrutiny of the brain not only warranted, but also refreshing.

As we proceed in the twenty-first century a major challenge and opportunity deals with our society's ability to manage advanced technologies and to apply new knowledge in practical ways to enhance the human condition. A clear example of this opportunity is our rapidly growing knowledge of the human brain. Our challenge and opportunity occurs on two fronts: first, we are challenged to increase our understanding of how the human brain works and how to maximize its function and utility. Second, we are challenged to develop practical approaches to enrich and enhance the human brain, thereby preventing or delaying onset of neurodegenerative conditions.

These two challenges are significant given the latest population estimates from the United States Census (US Census Bureau, 2001). More Americans are living longer than ever before. The latest census data indicates that approximately 39 million Americans are older than 64 years. The majority is female, numbering greater than 23 million while nearly 16 million men are 65 or older. The trend for Americans to live longer will continue, particularly as the health conscious baby-boomers begin to turn age 65 in the year 2010. The demographic shift of the United States certainly reflects a graying of the population. With an older America, information learned from ongoing brain research becomes paramount, particularly since dementia due to Alzheimer's disease is related to advanced age (Salmon & Bondi, 1997).

Perhaps as important as treating diseases of the brain in late life is the promotion of health and wellness across the lifespan. Health and wellness in late life is contingent upon health promoting lifestyles beginning in childhood, perhaps the womb, and continuing across the adult years (Nathanielsz, 1999). This premise is particularly true for brain health and it represents one of the major purposes for writing this book. In a direct appeal to the consumer, this book champions the idea that our brains not only have tremendous potential and capacity, but we possess a significant role in shaping the development and health of our brains across the entire lifespan.

Terminology

In order to communicate to others about the miraculous and complicated human brain, a clear language is needed. This language must be understood, not in academic terms, but in practical, user-friendly terms. As more individuals become interested and knowledgeable about the capacity of the human brain, there will be a greater likelihood of new methods, products, and approaches for brain enrichment across the lifespan. A review of the animal literature on brain function and structure provides the concept known as "neural plasticity." This seemingly complicated term has a multitude of meanings depending upon the context of its use. According to one source (Van Pragg, Kempermann, & Gage, 2000) Hebb proposed the conceptual framework for neuronal plasticity in the human brain in the late 1940s. He also was among the first to discuss the positive effects of an enriched environment on the structure and function of animal brains. Others (Kolb & Wishaw, 1998) contend the idea that experience can affect brain morphology may best be attributed to Ramon and Cajal.

Much laboratory-based research (Diamond & Hopson, 1998) on the relationship between environment and brain morphology in the animal model has emerged and is discussed in this book. The animal model helps us understand neural plasticity, particularly how environment helps to shape the animal brain. The more important issue for the purposes of this book, however, deals with the generalizability and application of such plasticity from animal-based brain research to the human brain. Generalizability enables development and implementation of health promoting behaviors for the human brain and perhaps prevention of neurodegeneration in late life.

For this book, neural plasticity (Gross, 2000) refers to the brain as a highly dynamic, constantly reorganizing, and unlimited system. Neural plasticity, as used in this text, therefore, confronts and refutes the long held belief that the human brain is fixed and limited from childhood (Gross, 2000), and incapable of neuronal generation (Rakic, 1985). Neuronal generation refers to birth of new brain cells and is one outcome of a system with plasticity.

Purpose and Structure of this Book

As declared earlier, a major purpose of this book is to advance the potential benefits of neural plasticity towards a human model of brain enrichment, prevention, and health and wellness. Reliable studies have been published on the relationship between environmental enrichment and brain development in the animal model (Diamond et al., 1964; Rosenzweig, Krech, Bennett, & Diamond, 1962). These studies have important implications for the human brain, particularly as we are now living longer, and as a society, appear to be increasingly interested in prevention and wellness. A new understanding of the human brain may spawn a dynamic developmental model for brain maturation and generation that far exceeds childhood, extending to the latter part of the lifespan.

The book begins with an historical perspective on the evolution and relatively recent emergence of neural plasticity as a new paradigm. The established ideas of brain development and brain structure are presented and contrasted with those of neural plasticity. The book then reviews the typical changes in human brain structure and function across the healthy lifespan to enable an understanding of the heterogeneity of the aging brain. While these changes are typical, the book entertains the possibility that changes in brain function and structure need not be degenerative only. With neural plasticity, there emerges a potential for continued development of brain structure and brain function across the lifespan. Literature on early life markers for prevention of late life neurodegeneration is presented to forward this case. An applied model of proactive health promotion and wellness for the human brain emerges from the paradigm of neural plasticity.

The burgeoning research in neurosciences prevents any book from completely reflecting the most current findings on the human brain. Nevertheless each published text and peer-reviewed manuscript adds to an ever-building knowledge base and may help to shape our understanding. This book is written to advance the current understanding of the human brain as established by so many scholars and scientists. The careers of these individuals have resulted in publications that explain the fundamentals of animal brain function, the importance of a nurturing and stimulating environment, and the potential similar effects upon the human brain. This book attempts to integrate these knowledge areas and to underscore the importance of an enriched and stimulating environment to the human brain. The book promotes the early brain-enriching environment as a direct trigger for lifelong brain health and potentially as a preventative mechanism against late life neurodegeneration. The practical implications from these ideas offer our nation's leaders the opportunity to adopt and promote more enlightened policies for human brain-health.

Chapter Two
Basics of the Human Brain

Given that this book deals primarily with the human brain we need to develop a working understanding of the basics of our brain. Many metaphors have been used to describe the human brain in an attempt to simplify our learning. Examples of such metaphors include the brain as a vast telephone network with multiple connections and wires. As the computer became more commonplace the metaphor of our brain working like a computer also became popular. The similarities of electrical connections and rapid transmission of information made this comparison attractive though flawed. Finally, the human brain has also been described as a universe similar to our own universe vast, complex, and mysterious.

As I travel the nation providing workshops on the human brain I try to make clear several critically important points to the audience: First, the human brain is the most complicated system ever to exist. It is far more sophisticated than any computer or robot that will ever be built in our lifetime and perhaps any lifetime. Second, the single greatest system ever built sits in our body within the thick tough shell known as the skull. Imagine, the most wonderful system is not only portable, but it travels with us wherever we go because it sits within the skull of our own body. Third, every human being should have a basic understanding of their brain. A working knowledge of the basics of brain structure and function will lead to a desire to care for and nurture our brain. To date, there not only is a significant lack of knowledge regarding the human brain by laypersons, there is very little momentum to change this unfortunate reality. Through my workshops and publications such as this book, I am trying to change that.

A fascinating fact about the human brain is that all of its complexity fits within a two to four pound structure. The human brain developed over time from the back to the front with regions near the base of the brain evolving first and the area of the brain just behind your forehead (frontal lobe) developing last. As such, the frontal lobe is the youngest region of the brain. The brain is comprised of billions of cells known as neurons (see Figure 1) and glial cells. Neurons are considered the true brain cells while glial cells maintain a supporting role. Neurons have a long arm known as an axon that sends information out to other neurons. The dendrites of a neuron are branch like figures that take information in from the environment. One neuron communicates by releasing a chemical (referred to as neurochemicals or neurotransmitters) that is received by another neuron (receptor cell). This chemical marriage is referred to as a synapse. From synaptic connections comes behavior, thought, and emotion. For purposes of this text the more synaptic connections we create in life the healthier our brains may be!

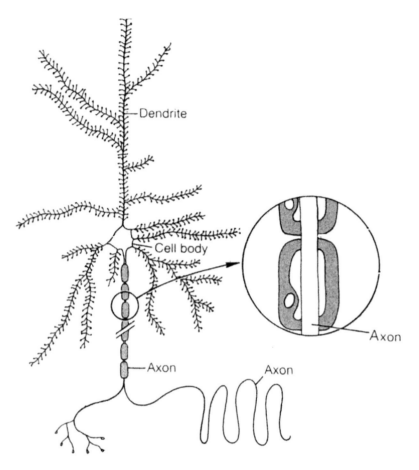

Figure 1. The human brain cell.

Equally interesting is the fact that although our brain weighs only about three pounds, it demands nearly 25% of the blood from every heart beat. This amazing fact is precisely why cardiopulmonary resuscitation is so important. Brain damage can occur within minutes of the heart not beating. These two vital parts of our being (heart and brain) work in a beautiful partnership and damage to the heart will likely have a negative effect on the brain. For purposes of this book this relationship underscores the importance of a healthy lifestyle not only for our hearts but for our brains. The interesting idea regarding a healthy lifestyle for the human brain as espoused by this book is that it will and should mimic the lifestyle already espoused as healthy for the heart. Indeed, it is my belief that our society needs to show as much love for our brain as we already do for our heart!

To assist our understanding, the brain can be organized in three primary ways. First, the brain has a cortex and subcortex. Cortex translates to mean "bark of a tree." For those who do not study the brain the cortex is the undulating "rumpled" structure that we all probably think of when we consider the brain. The cortex is the most sophisticated part of our brain, functions on a conscious level, and plays a critical role in our thinking, memory, language, judgment, orientation to space around us, personality, and abstract reasoning to name but a few functions. Neurons exist primarily in the cortex though not exclusively. Just under the cortex is a cluster of older, more primitive, and primarily motor-based structures collectively referred to as the subcortex. The subcortex evolved before the cortex, is more automatic and subconscious in nature, and serves to help us with smooth motor skills, swallowing, coordination, gait, balance, and speed of processing. The cortex and subcortex are two distinct regions of the brain but it is important to understand that they do not function in isolation. The brain is not a series of isolated instruments playing solo music. Rather the brain should be considered a symphony that integrates all structures into a functional harmony. Such is the case with the interplay between the cortex and subcortex.

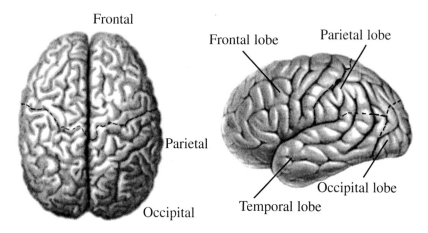

Figure 2. Two brain hemispheres and four lobes

A second organizational scheme is to consider the brain as having two hemispheres left and right (see Figure 2). For nearly all right handed dominant persons the left hemisphere is primarily responsible for language both expressive and receptive. The right hemisphere for these right handers has the primary responsibility of processing visuospatial information (orientation to the world around us), shapes, and sizes. Once again these hemispheres do not operate in isolation but rather as a symphony with communication occurring between the hemispheres. Such communication occurs across a cellular bridge known as the "corpus collosum." One third of left handers have an identical functional hemispheric organization as right handers. Approximately one third of left- handers, typically those who have a family history of left handedness have language distributed primarily in the right hemisphere while visuospatial skills are processed in the left hemisphere. The remaining third or so of left handers have functions distributed more equally in both hemispheres and do not necessarily adhere to the lateralized functions described above.

The third organizational structure of the human brain is regional with four distinct but interactive *lobes* identified. For each of these lobes there is a right and left lobe as expected given we have two hemispheres (see Figure 2). The occipital lobes are located in the most posterior part of the cortex and represent our primary visual center. The parietal lobes are located in front of the occipital lobes and help us with functions such as mental calculation and visuospatial orientation. Our temporal lobes sit just under our temples and are critically important for memory and learning. Indeed there is a well known structure deep in the middle part of each temporal lobe known as the "hippocampus" (see Figure 3). The hippocampus is critical for learning of new information and can be thought of as our brain's encoder. It takes new information in, rehearses such information, and permits a transmission of new information to permanent storage in the cortex itself. Without the hippocampus we would forget rapidly and be unable to form new memories. Interestingly, animal studies have demonstrated the hippocampus to generate new brain cells (neurogenesis) when exposed to environments that are enriched and stimulating. This will be reviewed in detail in the following chapters. The temporal lobes also help us comprehend what we hear and are considered our auditory center. Finally, the frontal lobes sit just behind our foreheads and represent the youngest and largest part of our brains. The frontal lobe is a complicated part of the brain that seems to help us with many different behaviors. Personality is thought to sit primarily in the frontal lobe. Complicated behaviors such as insight, planning, concept formation, judgment, and mental flexibility are subserved by the frontal lobes. Behavioral control and disinhibition are frontal lobe functions. Mood disorders and other psychiatric conditions such as schizophrenia, bipolar disorder, obsessive compulsive disorder, and attentional problems are thought to be related to frontal lobe dysfunction. As such I consider the frontal lobe to be the psychiatric department of the brain. It is important to maintain an understanding that the brain does not operate in regional silos but rather as a magnificent integrated system.

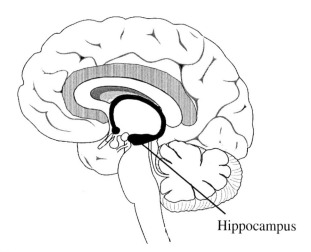

Hippocampus

Figure 3. The hippocampus (memory and learning)

We are not exactly sure how the brain takes in so much information and makes sense of it. However, consider how much information you are perceiving and processing at one time-both at the conscious and subconscious level-and the complexity of the system begins to emerge. It is interesting and important to consider how the brain is being affected by information that it processes. As the single greatest information processor ever created there still is a fundamental mystery regarding how the brain changes once information is processed. Further, we do not yet know for sure exactly how the brain processes information. Fundamental to this book is the emerging belief that the brain is not a rigid, fixed and limited system but rather a dynamic and reorganizing system. There is also new understanding that like animals our brains have capacity to change functionally and structurally though the mechanisms underlying this change are not yet known.

Early in his work Donald Hebb described changes that occur in the cells of the brain as a function of learning and exposure to stimulation. Change in function was related to change in structure that occurred at the cellular level. Development of new brain cells or development of new connections with existing brain cells are both theoretically possible though not conclusive. Similarly, we do not yet know if talents and new skills are born and stored in specific cells or distributed across regional networks of cells. In animal models studies have confirmed development of new brain cells in areas of the brain important to learning when these animals were exposed to stimulating environments. This book addresses the question of whether a similar relationship exists between environmental input and changes in brain structure and function in human beings. The study of animal brains is critical because there is similarity between the brains of animals and humans, particularly primates. Study of human brains is difficult because of obvious ethical issues (we cannot open the skulls of people and observe behavior unfolding in the brain). However, new neuroimaging procedures that provide a window of insight into the function of the brain without being invasive offer hope to more detailed study of our central nervous system. While the implications for neurogenesis in humans are enormous and research (described below) is emerging to support this idea more confidently, there is no conclusive and reliable evidence that the human brain develops new brain cells or new connections between existing brain cells.

An indirect method for arguing that the human brain has the same plasticity as animals is the emerging study of creativity across the lifespan (Cohen, 2001). Simply, creativity is found to manifest significantly in late life though the exact reason for this is not known. One theory might be that our frontal lobes that provide structure and inhibition to our behavior lose a disproportionate number of cells with normal aging (Squire, 1987). With such cell loss in the frontal lobes there is reason to believe creativity may emerge as a result of reduced inhibition and structure. There is almost a freedom for natural expression that may not exist at earlier stages of development. Regardless of the reason, the finding that creativity emerges in late life supports the idea that the human brain not only can change, but it can continue to develop and express new talents across the lifespan. It is difficult to imagine new talents at any age not having a neurophysiological cause and or effect. This would fit with findings from the animal model that indicate older animal brains have the capacity for neurogenesis.

The bottom line for most people who do not spend their careers studying the human brain is that we all need to learn the basics of brain structure and function. We all need to invest some time and energy in learning the current understanding of what promotes health of the brain and what may not. Further, we need to consider what types of behaviors fit into a lifestyle that potentially promotes the health and integrity of our brains and implement the lifestyle. While it is true that empirical evidence for a direct relationship between environmental stimulation (positive and negative) and change in structure and function of the human brain is not conclusive this book promotes the idea that a proactive lifestyle that includes specific behaviors may have a fundamentally important benefit to the health of our brains. This benefit may be preventative in nature or more modestly have a delaying effect on manifestation of brain disease.

Chapter Three
Neural Plasticity: A New Understanding of Brain Function

A recent review (Gross, 2000) aptly pointed out that the past century has been dominated by a central understanding in the field of neuroscience: new brain cells (neurons) do not grow in the brain of the adult mammal. Indeed, there was near complete acceptance that neurons develop only during the first several years of life and are not produced thereafter (Rakic, 1985). This understanding exists despite the assertion that the capacity of the adult human brain to produce new neurons (neurogenesis) had never been tested in any adult primate species prior to 1995 (Rakic, 1985).

The language of neuronal plasticity is complex and as noted above, this book will use the term *plasticity* to refer to the dynamic, constantly reorganizing, and malleable properties of the human central nervous system. *Neurogenesis* is used to describe production of new neurons, itself an outcome of neural plasticity. In 1949 Donald Hebb pioneered research on learning and memory at the cellular level. His theory that learning occurs upon the capacity of the neuron to be strengthened, changed, or associated with other cells from repeated activation is thought to represent the foundation for a model of plasticity in the central nervous system (Spatz, 1996). The clinical and practical relevance of a dynamic central nervous system can be regarded only as meaningful as the attention given to it, not only during early years of development, but also in the mature brain (Spatz, 1996).

The work of Hebb introduced critically important principles that appear to have been extraordinarily farsighted. The idea that the central nervous system is dynamic with capacity to change was a significant proposition. Further, the insight to question the presence of cellular plasticity beyond the presumed early years of development also represents a threshold for more far reaching investigation of the central nervous system. It is important to recognize the significance of these early ideas since they challenged many years of thinking about the brain, and also laid the foundation for the current re-emergence of neuronal plasticity.

Evolution of Neural Plasticity

The significance of the thinking espoused by Hebb can be appreciated if a brief historical perspective on our understanding and beliefs about the mammalian brain in the early part of the twentieth century is reviewed. According to Gross (2000), there was universal agreement at the turn of the nineteenth century that the brain of the adult mammal remained structurally constant. This idea of an unchanging adult brain in the mammal was fueled by studies in Europe that suggested neurogenesis in the adult brain did not occur because the structural components of the brain remained unchanged in appearance (Gross, 2000). Further, mitotic processes (cell division) had not been observed in the adult brain at that time further supporting the idea that neurogenesis does not occur beyond early life.

The early part of the twentieth century witnessed sporadic reports of neurogenesis beyond the early developmental periods of life (Gross, 2000). All of these studies involved animals such as rats and mice and reported neurogenesis from four days post-birth (Hamilton, 1901) to one-year-old rats (Bryans, 1959). A major problem with these and other reports of neurogenesis was the inability to differentiate the type of cells being generated. For example, it was not clear whether the undifferentiated cells were actually glial cells or neurons. As Gross (2000) pointed out, Ramon and Cajal's (1928) review of these early studies on potential neurogenesis suffered methodological problems limiting any ability to distinguish convincingly the multiplying glial cell from an actual neuron.

The development of specialized staining techniques permitted study of cell proliferation in the 1960s. One study (Smart, 1961) found neurogenesis in three-day-old mice, but could not replicate this finding in adult mice. Gross (2000) reviewed a series of studies (Altman, 1962; Altman, 1969; Altman & Das, 1965) that used staining procedures to demonstrate neurogenesis in the young and adult rat in the neocortex, dentate gyrus of the hippocampus, and the olfactory bulb. According to Gross (2000), the significance of these findings was generally ignored for two decades. Indeed, the prevailing view on neurogenesis in the adult mammal in 1970 was that no convincing evidence existed to support it (Jacobson, 1970). Nonetheless, the published studies by Altman, according to Gross (2000), were farsighted and deserving of increased attention.

The middle part of the 1980s found published support for the findings reported by Altman nearly two decades earlier. Using electron microscopy of 3H-thymidine labeled cells (chemical staining procedure to identify specific cells), Kaplan (1984) and Kaplan and Hinds (1977) demonstrated cells in the dentate gyrus and olfactory bulb of adult rats had the structural characteristics of neurons suggesting regenerative capacity. Kaplan (1981; 1985) then found evidence for neuronal development in the cerebral cortex of the adult rat. Finally, mitosis (division of identical chromosomes before the cell divides) was demonstrated in the subventricular zone (area below ventricles-fluid filled sacs of the brain) of the adult macaque monkey (Kaplan, 1984). Despite the significance of these studies, and their replication of previous research by Altman indicating the presence of neurogenesis in the adult mammal, the scientific community reportedly did not recognize the work (Gross, 2000).

A strong refutation of the work of Altman and Kaplan was forwarded by Rakic, (1985). Using postpubertal rhesus monkeys, given single and multiple injections of tritium-labeled thymidine (chemical staining procedure to highlight the presence of specific cells) and then killed three to six years later, no radiolabeled neurons were demonstrated. Rakic (1985) concluded that unlike neurons of some nonprimate species, all neurons of the rhesus monkey brain are produced during prenatal and early postnatal periods. Rakic (1985) speculated that the brains of primates might be limited in the ability for neurogenesis once adulthood is reached. Any prolonged period of interaction with the environment was thought to require a stable set of neurons to retain the acquired experiences in the synaptic pattern of connectivity. These points argued by Rakic reflect the original thoughts of the adult central nervous system being fixed and limited. Of interest, however, is the fact that the 1990s yielded more advanced imaging and radiologic staining procedures such that Rakic himself published evidence for neurogenesis in the dentate gyrus and olfactory bulb of the adult primate (Kornak & Rakic, 1999A). Such neurogenesis in the hippocampus and olfactory region of the adult primate was replicated in another study (Kornack & Rakic, 1999B), but despite these findings, Rakic maintained his original idea for limited neurogenesis in the adult primate. Further, the conclusion that neocortical neurons do not regenerate during the lifespan of macaque monkeys suggested humans demonstrate similar limitations. Kornack and Rakic (1999B) speculated that such limitations for adult neurogenesis might represent a significant impediment to replacement of neurons from trauma and dementia. Most recently, Rakic (2002) encouraged caution regarding cortical neurogenesis in the adult mammal, refuted findings for neurogenesis throughout the cortex of the adult animal because of methodological concerns, and called for credible evidence prior to discarding established historical arguments against neurogenesis.

Gross (2000) proposed three major reasons why the idea of neurogenesis finally emerged victorious against a century of thought supporting the fixed and limiting properties of the adult brain. First, a series of studies demonstrated convincingly neurogenesis in adult birds (Nottebohm, 1985; 1996). Second, new methods for labeling new cells that could distinguish neurons from glial cells were introduced. Third, neurogenesis was influenced by psychosocial factors such as stress, environmental enrichment, and hormones. The latter reason provided support for adult hippocampal neurogenesis that is dynamic and responsive to external stimuli. It is important to note, however, that general acceptance for neurogenesis as a major paradigm shift in our understanding of the central nervous system focused primarily on the dentate gyrus, a part of the hippocampus deep in the medial temporal lobe.

Conclusions for Neurogenesis in Primates

From the research reviewed above, there remains a strong debate in the field regarding the presence of neurogenesis in primates, particularly beyond early development. Most researchers seem to support the idea of rapid neuronal proliferation soon after birth. The time for such neuronal explosion may vary, but the fact that early infancy is a period for such neuronal development appears supported.

Clearly, neurogenesis in the primate adult is not supported universally. Some research has asserted cortical neurogenesis across the lifespan, while other research refutes such findings. One area of agreement across the research is the finding for neurogenesis in the adult primate within the hippocampal formation and the olfactory region. More specifically, the dentate gyrus of the hippocampus is an area that consistently demonstrates neurogenesis across the animal lifespan. There is less agreement for neurogenesis in other neocortical areas of the adult primate and a final answer is not yet available. Future research that is based on strong methodology and advanced histopathological examination should provide an answer.

Implications of Neural Plasticity

The existence of adult hippocampal neurogenesis is important because it first establishes the potential of neuronal plasticity beyond early years of maturation. Second, it enables discovery of the triggers for such neurogenesis, thereby beginning the process of developing an applied model for health promotion for the human brain. Turning again to findings from the animal model, Greenough, Cohen, & Juraska (1999) noted that in rodents, neurons continued to develop in the dentate gyrus of the hippocampus throughout adult life. These authors reviewed conflicting literature that supported this finding (Bayer, Yackel, & Puri, 1982; Kaplan & Hinds, 1977) and refuted it (Eckenhoff & Rakic, 1988). Within the past several years, Greenough and colleagues (1999) asserted that neurogenesis in adult life was revived by the finding of neurogenesis in the dentate gyrus of marmosets (Gould, Reeves, Graziano, & Gross,

1999C), adult macaque monkeys (Gould, Reeves, Fallah, Tanapat, Gross, & Fuchs, 1999B), and especially in humans (Eriksson et al., 1998). This latter study represents the first demonstration of neurogenesis in the human brain (studies to be discussed later) providing more interest regarding the potential for brain repair.

Environment and The Brain

Discovery of a trigger (s) for neurogenesis is critical as it enables development and implementation of methods and behaviors for expression of such triggers. Complexity of the environment has emerged as an important trigger to both proliferation and survivability of newly formed neurons in the animal (Beaulieu & Colonnier, 1987; Greenough et al., 1999). This fact, however, is not new and can be traced back to the early work of Marian Diamond who promoted the phrase "enriched environment" and published work demonstrating a direct relationship between environment and brain development of a rodent (Diamond, Krech, & Rosenzweig, 1964).

Interestingly, according to Diamond (Diamond & Hopson, 1998), the idea of an enriched environment was inspired by Donald Hebb who initially speculated that rats confined to small unstimulating cages developed brains deficient in problem solving compared to rats exposed to a stimulating environment. It was from this speculation that Diamond reportedly studied the idea of raising rats in two distinct kinds of cages: a large "enriched cage" filled with toys and with other rats; and a small "impoverishment cage" housing a solitary rat with no toys.

Using this methodology, Diamond and her research team discovered five basic principles of brain enrichment (Diamond & Hopson, 1998, page 31):

1. A stimulating and boring environment has a widespread effect throughout brain regions important to memory and new learning. Neurons in brain regions outside of the cortex respond by growing new dendrites or by shrinking.

2. For pregnant female rats, an enriched environment results in newborn pups with a thicker cortex compared to newborn pups born to impoverished females.

3. Nursing rat pups has an enrichment effect on the brain. Significant increases in cortical thickness results from exposure to enriched environments after only 1 week post-delivery. This is particularly true of the brain region important for sensory integration of environmental stimuli.

4. Environmental enrichment has a positive effect on cortical thickness on both infant and teenage rats. An impoverished environment, however, has a more significant negative impact—thinning effect on the cortex—than an exciting environment has on cortical thickness.

5. Brain changes occur in young adult rats, middle-aged rats, and in rats equivalent to a ninety-year-old human.

Since the early work on environmental enrichment by Diamond and her research team at California Berkeley, extensive research of the effects of environment on brain morphology has occurred. Enriched environments have contributed not only to cortical thickness in rodents, but also to neurochemical changes in the cerebral cortex (Rosenzweig, Krech, Bennett, & Diamond, 1962), to neuronal changes (number and size) in the hippocampus, an area important for memory and new learning (Kempermann, Brandon, & Gage, 1998; Kempermann, Kuhn, & Gage, 1997; Walsh & Cummins, 1979), to long term enhancement of synaptic strength or functionality of the hippocampus (Sharp, McNaughton, & Barnes, 1985), to glial activity (Soffie, Hahn, Terao, & Eclancher, 1999), synaptic formation and metabolic activity (Kolb & Wishaw, 1998), and to improved spatial memory (Nilsson, Perfilieva, Johansson, Orwar, & Erikkson, 1999).

More recently, neurogenesis in the hippocampus-dentate gyrus of the adult rodent has been reported after electroconvulsive therapy (Madsen, Treschow, Bolwig, Lindvall, & Tingstrm, 2000), with administration of lithium (Chen, Rajkowska, Du, Seraji-Bozorgzad, & Manji, 2000), with chronic antidepressant treatment (Malberg, Eisch, Nestler, & Duman, 2000), after traumatic brain injury (Dash, Mach, & Moore, 2001), and after transient global ischemia in the dentate gyrus of gerbils (Liu, Solway, Messing, & Sharp, 1998). These studies suggest that multiple types of environmental input to the brain may have a direct impact on the hippocampus and that "environmental enrichment" which typically includes expanded learning opportunities, increased socialization, more physical activity, and larger housing, may not completely explain this phenomenon. Neurogenesis, at least in rodents, mice, and gerbils may result from a compensatory effect where some damage to the brain has occurred. To this extent, there may be a type of internal enrichment in addition to the external enrichment of medication for example. It would appear our understanding about the type of environmental input and its specific or general impact on the animal and human brain across the organism's lifespan is not yet complete. In addition, the study of how mood disorders are associated with a reduction in neuronal and glial volume, how stress-induced atrophy and loss of hippocampal neurons may lead to depression, and how a seizure may enhance neurogenesis are intriguing questions currently receiving attention.

Other research indicates that physical activity alone from running not only increases cell proliferation and neurogenesis in the adult mouse dentate gyrus (Van Praag, Kempermann, & Gage, 1999), but also enhances learning and long-term potentiation in the dentate gyrus and hippocampus area CA1 (Van Praag, Christie, Sejnowski, & Gage, 1999). Interestingly, while socialization has been found to be an important variable for neurogenesis in the rodent model, social grouping alone does not account for the cerebral changes associated with environmental enrichment (Rosenzweig, Bennett, & Morimoto, 1978).

Non-Enriched Environments

In contrast to the positive effects of an enriched environment on neurogenesis, a deleterious or non-stimulating environment may lead to an underdevelopment of the central nervous system. Neuronal activity appears to be essential to the formation of a mature system of neural connections and may underlie the final arrangement of neural connections (Crair, 1999). To this extent, early life-environments may be quite important regarding the eventual maturation of the central nervous system. Behaviors such as neonatal handling of infant rats appear to limit the negative effects of glucocorticoid proliferation secondary to stress throughout their life (Meaney, Aitken, Van Berkel, Bhatnagar, & Sapolsky, 1998; Sapolsky, 1996). These authors assert that adrenal glucocorticoids may accelerate neuronal loss in the hippocampus and may be related to cognitive loss with advanced age. Similar to the findings by Meaney and colleagues (1998), maternal deprivation of infant rats was found to affect their behavior across the lifespan with particular deficits noted in learning (Francis & Meaney, 1999; Oitzl, et al., 2000). The relationship between prenatal stress, learning deficits, and inhibition of neurogenesis has been supported in other studies (Gould & Tanapat, 1999; Lemaire, Koehl, Moal, & Abrous, 2000). Interestingly, McEwen (1999) reported the hippocampus to be a target of stress hormones even though it is a brain region with capacity for neural plasticity and neurogenesis. This suggests there is both a plasticity and vulnerability to the hippocampus and that the type of environment (reduced stress) may be crucial for minimizing the vulnerability.

Chronic stress may accelerate age-related damage to the hippocampus with adrenal glucocorticoids likely triggering the damage (Smith, 1996). Stress has also been found to regulate neurotrophic factors expressed in the brain and in some cases to decrease the neurotrophic factor (Smith, 1996). Interestingly nerve growth factor and specific neurotrophins may actually increase when the central nervous system is exposed to stress and glucocorticoids (steroid hormone that affects the brain). Smith (1996) asserts that this may be a compensatory mechanism to stress-induced damage. Neurotrophic factors (factors that nurture development of brain cells) may protect the brain from insult and there is reason to hypothesize that they may also have a role in preventing or reversing glucocorticoid-damage to the hippocampus (Smith, 1996). Research to test this hypothesis is ongoing.

Neurogenesis in the Adult and Older Animal

Clearly, neurogenesis in mammals and non-human primates occurs. Novelty and complexity of the environment, socialization, and physical exercise are factors important to manifestation of neurogenesis. Handling of the infant also appears to be an important factor for neurogenesis perhaps by limiting the negative effects of stress-induced glucocorticoid proliferation. An important issue regarding neurogenesis in the animal deals with whether or not there is a critical period in the lifespan for neuronal development.

Prior to the middle part of the 1980s, it was reasonably accepted that the majority of neurons in the central nervous system in warm-blooded vertebrates developed in prenatal and early postnatal periods. For nonvertebrates such as fish, neurogenesis has been reported in adulthood (Birse, Leonard, & Coggeshall, 1983). An early demonstration of neurogenesis in the adult vertebrate (adult canary) was reported by Goldman & Nottenbohm (1983). Using adult canaries, Patton and Nottenbohm (1984) replicated neuronal generation in the adult central nervous system. Further, these authors demonstrated that central nervous system cells that develop in adulthood have the capacity to adopt a neuronal morphology, to show synaptic and action potentials, and to be recruited into functional circuits.

More recently, research has focused on the impact of aging upon experience dependent hippocampal neurons. In older rats, there is attenuation in the ability of the hippocampus to transmit spatial information when compared to younger rats (Shen, Barnes, McNaughton, Skaggs, & Weaver, 1997). These authors speculated that reduced functional plasticity within the hippocampus in late life might represent a significant factor in age-related memory impairment.

The contribution of an enriched environment has also been studied with regard to neurogenesis and synaptic plasticity in the hippocampus in late life. Compared to mice and rats living in standard cages, older mice and rats living in enriched environments demonstrate significantly more neurons in the dentate gyrus of the hippocampus (Kempermann, Kuhn, & Gage, 1998) and synaptic strengthening (Nakamura, Kobayashi, & Ohashi (1999). The Kempermann et al., (1998) study supports the presence of a complex regulatory mechanism for production of neurons in the dentate gyrus in the aging brain and strengthens the idea that plasticity in the older brain has functional benefits. Findings from research on experience-dependent plasticity have been applied to promote child development, successful aging, and even recovery from brain damage (Rosenzweig & Bennett, 1996).

Greenough, Cohen, and Juraska (1999) reviewed the mechanism by which experience regulates neurogenesis in the adult rodent hippocampus. Neurogenesis in adult life is significant for it may imply brain repair, and research has demonstrated that both proliferation and survival of newly formed neurons can be affected by experience (Gould, Beylin, Tanapat, Reeves, & Shors, 1999A; Van Pragg, Kempermann, & Gage, F. 1999). The mechanism serving survival rate of neurons in the hippocampus is dependent on learning that involved the hippocampus. Survival of neurons was reduced with hippocampus-independent learning.

According to Greenough and colleagues (1999), hippocampal learning is critical for neuronal survival, and new neurons are more dependent on activity than mature neurons. There may be a critical period for neuronal survival and dependency on activity that occurs shortly after formation. Gould and colleagues (1999A) suggested this critical period because soon after neuronal formation occurs, axons emerge from the dentate gyrus and begin to contact target cells in specific hippocampal sublayers.

Proliferation of newly formed neurons also appears to occur within a critical period if the rodent is exposed to an activity such as physical exercise (Van Pragg et al., 1999). The increased activity not only increases proliferation of new neurons in the hippocampus, but also increases survivability of existing neurons in the same region. The hippocampus, therefore, becomes a critically important brain structure when trying to understand neurogenesis. The hippocampus has a unique capacity to regulate the production of new neurons from continuously generated precursor cells (cells the precede brain cells). Recent research demonstrates similar neurogenesis to also occur in the neocortex of adult primates (Gould, Reeves, Graziano, & Gross, 1999C; Sanjay, Leavitt, & Jeffrey, 2000).

According to Greenough and colleagues (1999), the hippocampus is critically important for encoding new information. It also has a capacity to form short-lived representations permitting reactivation of similar or identical representations in the cerebral cortex. This mechanism serves to prevent an interference effect when our brain processes new information and learns sequentially without obscuring existing information. Such a functional capacity would render the hippocampus important for new learning and for contribution to permanent storage of previously learned information. These functional abilities, therefore, would require the hippocampus to have a significant role in both the production and survival of neurons.

Another view of the unique functional capacity of the hippocampus suggests that it may have distinct neurons for encoding of new information from those that process more obsolete information (Greenough et al. 1999). The hippocampus might play an important role within the entire cerebral cortex by facilitating new learning and by avoiding interference with distinct neurons that aid in the storage of older information. If the hippocampus has such a dual capacity, there is clearly an adaptive and complex value unlike any other known brain structure. The mechanisms underlying hippocampal neurogenesis and promotion of survivability of existing neurons (plasticity) would be critical and necessary to process information as described.

Learning has been proposed as a neurobiological function important to neurogenesis in the adult animal (Gould, Tanapat, Hastings, & Shors, 1999D). While the functional significance of such neurogenesis remains unclear, there are consistent findings demonstrating the link. Hippocampal dependent learning (learning as a consequence of normal function of the hippocampus) is affected negatively by stress, advanced age, and steroids such as glucocorticoids while positive effects include estrogen and living in an enriched environment (Gould et al., 1999D). Adult generated neurons are affected by and may be involved in hippocampal dependent learning and the mechanisms underlying this together with the adaptive significance are now under study.

Continuous generation of neurons in the hippocampal dentate gyrus of adult and old macaque monkeys, though significantly less than that demonstrated in the young adult rodent dentate gyrus, suggests the presence of potent neural stem cell(s) is(are) retained in the adult primate hippocampus (Gould, Reeves, Fallah, Tanapat, Gross, & Fuchs, 1999B; Kornak & Rakic, 1999A). Neural stem cells have been identified in the adult mammalian central nervous system (Johansson, Momma, Clarke, Risling, Lendah, & Frisen, 1999) and are thought to be a type of factory for development of brain cells. Stimulation from the environment early in life may preserve a potential for neurogenesis in the dentate gyrus and the novelty of complex stimuli (not simply continuous complex stimuli) may be the most critical factor from the environment upon adult hippocampal neurogenesis (Kempermann & Gage, 1999).

Adult neurogenesis in nonhuman primates offers a good model to investigate neurogenesis in humans and to the significance of plasticity in the adult brain. Macaque monkeys have similar phylogenic characteristics to humans, have similar long life spans, and also have complex cognitive abilities (Kornak & Rakic, 1999A). Again, these authors and others (Sanjay et al., 2000) underscore the practical significance of neurogenesis in adult humans as new therapeutic strategies may emerge to replace neurons lost to brain trauma, stroke, and other neurodegenerative diseases. As study of neurogenesis in humans is presently difficult, some (Gould et al., 1999C; Kornak & Rakic, 1999A) have proposed the use of macaque monkeys who have similar hippocampal formations to humans.

Conclusions for Environment & Neurogenesis

Overall, while the idea of neurogenesis in the adult primate has generated significant research indicating neuronal development in hippocampal and neocortical (most recently developed area of the brain translated to mean "new cortex") association areas (Gould et al., 1999C), some present more cautious interpretations of the research (Nowakowski & Hayes, 2000). Such debate can make difficult research exploring the functional capacity of new neurons that Gould and Gross (2000) assert can be conducted through a combination of behavioral, selective lesion, ultrastructural, and electrophysiological studies. The generalizability of findings from animal and non human primate models of neurogenesis to humans remains important though inconclusive.

What is significant, however, is the importance of environmental input and enrichment value to a developing brain. The importance of the environment on structural and functional properties of the brain may be independent of research that attempts to measure neurogenesis from histopathological staining procedures. A critical factor and perhaps confound to such research that supports or refutes neurogenesis in the neocortex (new brain or most recently developed area of the brain) of the adult primate is the type of environment the organism has been exposed. There is enough evidence to assert that the enrichment value of the environment has a direct role on the presence or absence of neurogenesis in the hippocampus of the adult and older adult animal. The same may be true for areas of the brain outside of the hippocampus. Any investigation on neurogenesis must account for environmental exposure. Clearly, the importance of environment on brain development and morphology must also be considered when investigating human brain development and degeneration.

Chapter Four
Neurogenesis in Humans

The research on neurogenesis in animals, including non-human primates is rather convincing in its demonstration of the plasticity of the central nervous system. This includes neurogenesis in adulthood and in later adulthood. Clearly, the complexity and novelty of the environment are two critical factors related to neurogenesis in the animal. Other significant factors that contribute to the richness of the environment include socialization, touch, and physical activity. While the demonstration of neurogenesis in the animal brain is an important finding, the generalizability of such neurogenesis to the human central nervous system, and specifically, the hippocampus, remains at present inconclusive (Rakic, 2002). It is important to note, however, that with more advanced neuroimaging and more sophisticated chemical staining procedures, evidence is emerging to support neurogensis in the human brain.

Neurogenesis in the adult brain was refuted by Rakic (1985) who asserted no study of adult primates had been published to determine the capacity to generate new neurons. Rakic (1985) noted the published reports of both replacement and addition of neurons in the brains of adult fish, amphibians, birds, and rodents had led to speculation that neurogenesis may occur in the human adult. Using twelve rhesus monkeys ranging in age from 6 months to 11 years, Rakic (1985) found that the full compliment of neurons in the primate central nervous system was attained shortly after birth. This finding differed from the variable pattern of post-developmental neurogenesis in nonprimate species. Rakic speculated that the brain of primates is uniquely specialized in lacking the ability to produce neurons upon reaching adulthood. Human neurogenesis was argued to follow a pattern of time-limited neurogenesis with such neuron proliferation occurring shortly after birth (Kotulak, 1997; Rakic, 1985).

More recent research demonstrates neurogenesis in the cortex and hippocampal formation of adult primates including old-world primates (Gould et al., 1999B; Gould et al., 1999C; Kornak & Rakic, 1999A; Kornak & Rakic, 1999B). The monkey brain similar to the human provides a model for neurogenesis in the human central nervous system and hope for regeneration of areas damaged from stroke and other neurodegenerative diseases. Neurogenesis and neural plasticity presents a paradigm that stands in contrast to traditional thinking in neurobiology that the mature brain cannot produce new nerve cells. Similarly, the long held beliefs that adult neurogenesis is a feature unique to less advanced animals and not possible in primates and humans because of the complexity of their brains have been refuted (Kempermann & Gage, 1998). Clearly, one could argue that the sophisticated and highly complex central nervous system of humans should have at a minimum the same capacity for neurogenesis as rodents and pigs!

As noted earlier in this book the study of neurogenesis in humans is more difficult than similar study of animals. For one, human brains cannot be selected for study and analyzed for neurogenesis for obvious ethical reasons that do not limit such study with animals. Second, the traditional thought about the human brain as a generally fixed and limited system not capable of neurogenesis has been entrenched for many years. Any shift in such a relatively fixed scientific mindset will not change easily or quickly. Finally, our advancement in technology, primarily in neuroimaging procedures that provide real-time in vitro functional analysis has occurred recently. We still do not have sophisticated noninvasive technology for studying changes at the cellular (neuronal) level and rely on chemical staining procedures of cells taken at biopsy or autopsy. As our technology for the study of the brain increases we will learn much more about the cellular aspects of the brain, brain physiology and the effect from the environment, and thereby be better able to support or refute neurogenesis in humans.

A potentially groundbreaking study in support of human neural plasticity (Eriksson et al., 1998) reported neurogenesis in the hippocampus of the human brain. This is precisely the same critical brain region found to have the capacity for neurogenesis in the animal brain. According to these authors, demonstration of neurogenesis in the adult human brain had not occurred prior to their publication. Regions of the adult human brain previously shown to be neurogenic in adult rodents and monkeys were examined for neurogenesis. Human brain tissue was examined postmortem from five cancer patients treated with DNA labeling for neuron markers. New neurons, as defined by these markers, were generated from dividing progenitor cells within the dentate gyrus of the hippocampus in adult humans, the same brain region found to evince neurogenesis in many other species. Eriksson and colleagues (1998) argued that the human hippocampus-dentate gyrus, similar to rodents, retains the ability for neurogenesis throughout life.

Eriksson and colleagues (1998) point out that while the results from their study indicate the adult human brain undergoes cell division and that some of these cells survive and further differentiate into neurons, their work has not demonstrated support that these new cells are functional. Further, these authors admit they do not yet understand the biological significance for neurogenesis in the adult human brain. Overall, this study is promoted as one that now provides a foundation for further investigation of neuroplasticity in humans with an emphasis on addition of neurons across the lifespan. Eriksson and colleagues (1998) offer examples of such further investigation to include in vitro and in vivo studies of cell differentiation and potential transplantation studies. Further, since studies have already demonstrated a positive relationship between environmental stimulation and neurogenesis in the adult and older animal, there is potential to regulate similar neurogenesis in humans. The latter point is the underlying message of this text.

This study provided the first evidence for neurogenesis in the human brain, heretofore considered impossible. More recent research on temporal lobe tissue (location of hippocampus and dentate gyrus) from humans status-post temporal lobectomy also supports neurogenesis in the adult human hippocampus (Roy et al., 2000). Further, neural plasticity in the human brain has support from a demonstration of synaptic plasticity in the human hippocampus similar to that found in rodents and potentially critical to declarative memory (Beck, Goussakov, Lie, Helmstaedter, & Egler, 2000). While additional evidence for human neurogenesis is needed prior to drawing firm conclusions, these findings offer initial evidence that the human brain has similar regenerative capacities as animals and non-human primates. The region of neurogenesis established in animal brains appears to be identical to that asserted by recent studies of neurogenesis in humans. Further, these studies offer significant interest because regenerative capacity and repair in the human brain becomes possible with neurogenesis.

Important recent research on neural stem cells (specialized cells that serve to produce other cells such as brain cells) indicates that while the majority of cells in the central nervous system of mammals are born during embryonic and early post-natal periods, new neurons continue to be added in certain regions of the adult mammalian brain (Johansson et al., 1999). The new brain cells are derived from a group of stem cells that may be propagated in vitro if taken from the adult brain (Reynolds & Weiss, 1992). Stem cells have the capacity for self-renewal and the ability to generate major classes of neural cells such as neurons and glial cells (cells that nurture and support neurons) (Reynolds & Weiss, 1996).

Interestingly, neural stem cells have recently been

isolated from the walls of the ventricular system of the adult mammalian central nervous system and hippocampus (see Johansson et al., 1999). These ependymal cells (produce fluid for the brain and insulate the brain's ventricles-fluid filled sacs) make up the wall of the ventricular system and it is these ependymal cells (at least some percentage of them) that are believed to be the neural stem cells (Johansson et al., 1999). These authors assert that the ependymal cells divide rarely, but after an injury the proliferation rate increases with progeny directed to the site of the injury and eventual differentiation to astrocytes. As Johansson and colleagues (1999) report, our understanding of how the molecular mechanisms triggering proliferation of neural stem cells after injury occurs may offer insights to methods for stimulating neurogenesis. Such understanding can lead to neurogenesis from utilization of endogenous stem cells in the treatment of neurodegenerative conditions. This treatment approach would appear to have advantages over transplantation of cells from animals or human embryos as the latter approach is ripe with ethical and immunological concerns.

Human Brain Development: Measuring Changes in Behavior

Neural plasticity and neurogenesis in the human brain is an area of tremendous importance. Research is ongoing to build upon the significant findings of Eriksson and colleagues (1998) and there is good reason to believe that the relationship between environment and brain morphology that exists in the animal brain will also be demonstrated for the human brain. A human central nervous system with capacity to regenerate neurons would represent a new horizon for health promotion and potentially other areas important to the human condition.

Another avenue to explore the potential plasticity of the human central nervous system is to review the developmental literature. Similar to the traditional ideas that argue against plasticity in the human brain, there is an established belief that the human brain has a certain fixed time period for "critical development." In his review of the emerging literature on this topic, Kotulak (1997) presented an argument for the importance of early learning within a stimulating environment. While it may not be overtly stated, there is an entrenched belief that the human brain does not produce new brain cells after childhood and that brain cells are only lost across the lifespan. Such ideas indicate a human central nervous system that is highly fixed, limited, and degenerative.

These ideas have drawn recent scrutiny and new ideas regarding human brain development might offer a perspective more consistent with the model of neural plasticity. Cognition is one outcome of brain function that can be measured across the lifespan. Within the past 75 years new ideas regarding cognitive capacity and skill acquisition across the lifespan have emerged. Early research (Wechsler, 1958) suggested a decline in general intelligence with advanced age. Particular deficits were noted in nonverbal intelligence, thought to be less influenced by information learned in school. Indeed, intelligence for academic-based information was labeled "crystallized intelligence" (Horn

& Catell, 1967) while information thought to be more vulnerable to age-effects was labeled "fluid intelligence (Horn & Catell, 1967)." This research was deemed problematic, as the methodology employed was cross-sectional. Cross-sectional research compared the intellectual abilities of older adults to younger adults resulting in a predictable advantage for the younger adults. As a result, the issue of intellectual change across the lifespan was not adequately addressed.

Longitudinal research that measures a given behavior in a sample of persons over time revealed a more accurate picture of intelligence in advanced age. Using longitudinal methodology, age-effects on intelligence were less pronounced. According to Schaie (1990), intellectual development is sustained until the sixth decade of life. Thereafter, there appears to be decline, though variability appears to be a rule and not the exception. A primary contributing factor to intellectual decline in advanced age is medical illness (Albert & Moss, 1988; Schaie, 1990). Longitudinal studies are flawed to the extent they may overestimate abilities secondary to attrition of less healthy and motivated subjects.

Additional reviews (La Rue, 1992; Nussbaum, 1998) indicate that different general cognitive abilities change at different age periods in a healthy central nervous system. For example, language appears to withstand the effects of age rather well until the seventh and even eight decade of life. In contrast, memory for new information may begin to show even subtle change closer to the sixth decade of life. General intelligence, as noted above, demonstrates earlier changes in processing of nonverbal, non-academic based information. Interestingly, personality has been shown to demonstrate stability late into life (Starratt & Peterson, 1998).

The art and the science of measuring and reflecting cognitive change in an older person with a healthy central nervous system remain difficult. There is much overlap in expected cognitive changes between healthy older persons and those older persons with mild medical or neuropsychiatric illnesses (Wilson, Bennett, & Swartzendruber, 1998). Indeed, these authors indicate the differential remains an imperfect science and caution is indicated when attempting to make such distinctions. Of interest, however, is that most of the research indicates variability in cognitive abilities across the lifespan, with more variability with more advanced age, a finding that is consistent with a plastic or flexible central nervous system.

Some (Snowdon, 2001; Whalley, 2001) have argued a distinction between the processes underlying illness from that underlying aging. Indeed, these authors remind us that persons living into their ninth and tenth decades of life may be healthier and more cognitively intact than peers many years younger. Risk of major life-threatening diseases tends to decrease by the middle part of the ninth decade. The fact that many Americans alive in their nineties and beyond maintain such healthy central nervous systems presents a valuable population base for study of the healthy brain.

Measuring Changes in Brain Structure

The structure of the brain is another brain characteristic that may be measured across the lifespan. According to Powers (1994), structural changes of the human brain begin around the fifth decade of life, similar to the time when some cognitive changes occur. Although the brain weighs approximately 1450 grams at maturity, it loses nearly 100 grams by the 75th year of life (Kolb & Wishaw, 1990). Brain weight has been shown to decline across the lifespan, though similar to cognitive change, variability exists (Dekaban & Sadowsky, 1978; Snowdon, 2001). Other research suggests the white matter of the healthy brain is particularly vulnerable to cell loss with advanced age (Coffey & Figiel, 1991), particularly in the oldest of persons (Salat, Jeffrey, & Janowski, 1999). Cortical areas particularly vulnerable to cell loss or atrophy include the hippocampus (Powers, 1994) and prefrontal regions (Squire, 1987).

Ventricular size is a brain structure that may be measured across the lifespan. According to Albert and Moss (1988) who reviewed the literature on computerized tomography (CT) and aging, ventricular size (size of the fluid filled sacs in the brain) increases across the lifespan. However, there is no convincing evidence regarding the age of onset for increased ventricular size with ages ranging from 40 to 60. According to more recent investigation (Bigler, 1997), a steady decline in total brain volume with a related increase in cerebral spinal fluid occurs with advanced age. It is thought that the decline in overall brain mass may begin around the fourth decade of life with a linear pattern of decline that speeds up in senescence (Bigler, 1997).

The decline in brain volume is thought to correlate well with the changes in cognition noted above.

Turning to more recent research of structural changes in the brain across the lifespan, men between the third and fifth decade of life demonstrate a consistent decline in hippocampal measured volume compared to women (Pruessner, Collins, Pruessner, & Evans, 2001). The head and tail of the hippocampus were particularly vulnerable to cell loss. The change in hippocampal volume is consistent with other recent research demonstrating that changes in gray matter begin earlier and result in a larger volume loss in men compared to women (Coffey et al., 1998). That cells are destined to die within the human hippocampus as we age receives some refute from Whalley (2001) who reviews research offering a greater role for neurochemical changes and memory change.

Important to the whole issue of critical periods of brain development that begin and end in childhood, recent research suggests the concept of a critical period defined by a limited age might be invalid. Two studies (Giedd et al., 1999; Sowell et al., 1999) using sophisticated magnetic resonance imaging technology, demonstrates continued brain maturation in the frontal neocortex well into the second decade of life. These authors argued for the relationship between the continued structural developments with cognitive development during this time period in life. Additionally, longitudinal measures indicate linear increases in white matter, but non-linear changes in cortical gray matter suggesting parietal lobe and frontal lobe peaking at age 12, temporal lobe at age 16, and an increase in occipital lobe development through age 20 (Giedd et al., 1999). Some of these changes occur at least one year earlier for females compared to males, suggesting the potential for a hormonal contribution. Finally, a recent study using magnetic resonance imaging (MRI) technology in a sample of adult men found the adult human brain continues to express periods of maturation in the white matter into the fifth decade of life followed by degeneration (Bartzokis et al., 2001). This latter study adds to the scrutiny now placed on the concept of critical periods to brain development, particularly those that assert such development occurs only in childhood.

Indeed, the concept of critical periods for human brain development is presently under scrutiny. Thompson and Nelson (2001) suggest consideration for "sensitive periods" rather than critical periods to reflect a broader and more flexible time period. These authors also point out that much of our attention and that of the media on brain development have been on the early years of childhood. They caution this approach and instead suggest attention be given to brain development across the lifespan. With continued study of the human brain using more advanced neuroimaging technologies, the development of the brain beyond adolescence may be due to factors separate from those that originate in childhood. Overall, Thompson and Nelson (2001) assert that our understanding of human brain development is in its infancy.

Conclusions for Human Brain Changes and Aging

One of the most salient and heuristic findings from

research on the human brain across the lifespan is variability. Such variability appears to increase with advanced age and suggests factors other than age itself may account for structural, chemical, and functional changes. The presence of variability also supports the idea for plasticity in the human central nervous system. Those factors most important to healthy, productive brains late in life probably include environment, illness, and lifestyle. Similar to the research on animals that established the importance of enriched and non-enriched environments to brain morphology, the human brain is most likely directly affected by environmental input.

A lifespan model to human brain health indicates the importance of environmental input from the earliest periods of life to the last stages of life. Research on sensitive periods for human brain development suggests the possibility for brain development beyond early childhood. Neuroimaging research also supports the idea for continued brain development and growth beyond childhood. Cognitive capacity is maintained late into life and new talents and skills continue to emerge at all ages. These findings support a highly plastic and capable central nervous system in humans that may require a new conceptual approach to our understanding of human brain development and potential.

To date, the human brain has traditionally been studied as a system rich in complexity and development primarily in early life. Beyond such neuronal development in childhood, human brain functioning has been considered from a model of decline and disease. With neural plasticity and the promise of neurogenesis in the hippocampus and perhaps other cortical regions, a model of human brain productivity and enrichment might be more appropriate.

Factors necessary to promote brain development and brain health across the lifespan can be identified and implemented. Such factors may present early in life and be necessary building blocks towards development of a healthy brain. Adverse factors in life such as parental deprivation and poverty may represent triggers for brain illness and neurodegeneration. Turning to the robust findings of the environmental enrichment model from animal studies on brain development, a similar model for the human brain is encouraged and timely. We can view the human brain from a health perspective and promote early environmental input to foster brain development and growth across a lifespan. Such a proactive model for the human brain not only promotes health, but may also limit triggers for neurodegenerative illnesses.

Chapter Five
Implications of Neural Plasticity for the Aging Brain

The first several chapters of this book introduced the concept of neural plasticity and neurogenesis as articulated in research on animals. For purposes of this book, neural plasticity infers a brain that is highly dynamic, constantly reorganizing, and malleable. Neurogenesis is but one outcome of a brain that has the property of plasticity. Animal research demonstrates convincingly that neurogenesis occurs in the brains of animals and perhaps more importantly in primates well into adulthood.

That rats and other animals have the capacity to regenerate brain cells is not merely of academic interest. Neurogenesis offers potential for both brain development and brain repair. While the human brain has not convincingly demonstrated such capacity, new evidence suggests our brains have the capacity for neurogenesis (Eriksson et al., 1998). The implications for neurogenesis in the aging human brain are striking and represent the focus of this chapter.

While the vast science on human brain function and structure historically has championed a central nervous system that is fixed, limited, and in progressive decline after adolescence, increased scrutiny has surfaced to challenge these ideas (Gross, 2000). Indeed, it is not uncommon to read references to the traditional view of human brain capacity as "dogma" (see Gross, 2000) and to witness declarations of the death of such beliefs. Today, our understanding of the human central nervous system is undergoing a paradigm shift that emphasizes neural plasticity as the primary conceptual basis for brain development into adulthood (Gross, 2000). The resulting intellectual tension has resulted in a direct confrontation between the traditional view of the human brain and the new paradigm that underscores neural plasticity. Of significance is the fact that traditional views are being challenged and new evidence to support the argument for neural plasticity is being published (Eriksson et al., 1998). Whether the emerging momentum for neural plasticity in the human brain is maintained by empirical research remains unknown. Nonetheless, we have learned a significant amount about neural plasticity from the animal model to begin making some generalizations to the human brain.

The cortex (Diamond et al., 1978) and hippocampus (Kempermann & Gage, 1999), an important structure for learning new information and sustaining learned information, have capacity for neurogenesis in the animal model. Environmental stimulation in the form of learning (Gould, Beylin, Tanapat, Reeves, & Shors, 1999A), physical stimulation such as running (Van Pragg et al., 1999), socialization

(Rosenzweig et al., 1978), and general enrichment (Diamond & Hopson, 1998) has demonstrated a direct morphological effect on the brain of animals. As noted above, particular attention has been given to the well-replicated finding of neurogenesis in the hippocampus of animals.

In contrast, research with animals has revealed delayed maturation of the animal brain when the early environment is stressful (Lemaire et al., 2000; Smith, 1995) and lacking maternal attention (Francis & Meaney, 1999; Oitzel et al., 2000). The production and proliferation of steroid hormones in the developing animal exposed to chronic stress is believed to have a negative effect on the brain and hippocampus in particular (Gould & Tanapat, 1999; McEwen, 1999; Meaney et al., 1988; Smith, 1996). Animals exposed to early environments with significant stress undergo high production of steroid hormones and demonstrate learning deficits that might last across their lifespan (Gould & Tanapat, 1999; Lemaire et al., 2000; Meaney et al., 1988).

Without doubt, the research reviewed in earlier chapters and briefly re-introduced above, indicates a direct relationship between environment and brain development in animals. This relationship dates back to the early 1960s (Altman & Das, 1964; Bennett, Diamond, Krech, & Rosenzweig, 1964) and has been replicated many times (Van Pragg, Kempermann, & Gage, 2000). Animals raised in and exposed to environments rich in stimulation, novelty, and complexity demonstrate brains that are better developed than those animals not exposed to such environments (see Diamond & Hopson, 1998). As noted above, impoverished environments have the opposite effect, inhibiting brain development. Perhaps as important, the effects of the early environment on the developing brain appear to be sustaining across the lifespan (Diamond & Hopson, 1998; Lemaire et al., 2000).

Enrichment is the term employed to describe environments that include a combination of complex inanimate and social stimulation (Rosenzweig et al., 1978). The relevance of any single factor is difficult to determine, though the combination of environmental factors appear to be essential for an environment to be enriched. In the experimental setting, an environment is considered enriched in relation to standard laboratory housing conditions. Enriched environments include larger cages, larger groups of animals, and more opportunity for more complex socialization. Voluntary physical activity is also more available to animals exposed to enriched environments compared to standard housing.

Environmental Enrichment and the Brain

Cognitive theories have been proposed to explain how environmental enrichment might affect the central nervous system. One theory is known as the arousal hypothesis that suggests animals become aroused when confronted with a new and complex environment (Walsh & Cummins, 1975). A second theory known as the learning and memory hypothesis (Rosenzweig & Bennett, 1996) suggests the action of morphological change occurs at the cellular level where learning occurs. This theory has support from the large amount of research demonstrating neurogenesis in the hippocampal structure (the structure critical to learning and memory) of animals exposed to enriched environments.

The exact mechanism underlying the effects of enriched environment upon brain morphology remains unknown. The learning and arousal explanations are not conclusive and appear to have varying level of support (Van Pragg, Kempermann, & Gage, 2000). Voluntary physical exercise such as running in a wheel increased both cell proliferation and recruitment of new neurons into the dentate gyrus of the hippocampus (Van Pragg, Kempermann, & Gage, 1999) suggesting physical activity is also a critical factor of the enriched environment. Different experiences might also result in similar anatomical and physiological changes. This process might suggest common final pathways of cellular and molecular events underlying different experiences. However, Kempermann and colleagues (1999) indicate that this process might also reveal our limited understanding of the neurobiology of behavior. Nonetheless, these authors suggest that physical exercise alone might be the critical factor for neural changes within an enriched environment because all measures affected by such environments have not been dissociated from exercise.

Clearly, the environment has an important contribution to brain development in animals, and there appears to be multiple types of stimuli in the environment that are enriching. The exact mechanism for the relationship between the brain development and environmental enrichment, however, remains unclear. Further, the precise contribution of different elements of the environment upon this change in brain morphology is unknown.

Nonetheless, our lack of understanding does not minimize the significance of a direct relationship between environment and brain structure and function. It is this critical relationship that enables some critical thinking regarding the potential importance of environmental contributions to human brain development.

Environmental Enrichment: Animals to Humans

It is important to note that there is no conclusive empirical replication for the environmental effects upon brain morphology in humans that exists in animals including primates. Nonetheless, the research on the impact (positive and negative) of environment upon animal brain structure and brain function across the lifespan has substantial empirical support to begin generating similar concepts for the human brain. The demonstration of neurogenesis in the human brain (Eriksson et al., 1998) provided a critical finding that supports further investigation and consideration for environmental enrichment on the human brain. Specifically, this study found the human brain to possess capacity for neurogenesis in the hippocampus, the same structure found in animals. A system that has the capacity for neurogenesis is inherently plastic and therefore may be modified by environmental input.

It is more than reasonable to consider the importance of early environments upon the development of the human central nervous system. Research (Diamond & Hopson, 1998; Kotulak, 1997; Mortensen, Michaelsen, Fleisher, Sanders, & Reinisch, 2002) has documented evidence on the importance of early environments upon cortical and psychosocial development. These authors have been instrumental in igniting and sustaining the importance of environment upon brain function and structure in the human. Extrapolating from the animal model, early environments rich in parental nurturing, nutrition, stimulation, socialization, and exercise might have beneficial effects for the human brain (Kotulak, 1997; Mortensen et al., 2002). These effects may be long lasting, serving as a neuronal boost that fosters brain development into adulthood. Clearly, recent research indicates development in the human brain continues into adulthood, well beyond previous understanding (Bartzokis et al., 2001). In addition, the idea for critical periods of human brain development limited to the first several years of life is now under direct challenge (Thompson and Nelson, 2001).

Animal research that indicates stressful environments early in life have negative effects on brain structure and function due to adrenal gland steroid proliferation may also have import for the human. The hippocampus is a vulnerable structure to such steroid proliferation that leads to learning deficits and spatial memory deficits in animals as reported above. For humans, chronic stress manifested as post-traumatic stress disorder (PTSD) has been reported (Sapolosky, 1998) to demonstrate MRI-based structural changes in the hippocampus of humans compared to controls. This finding, though clearly in need of replication, indicates another piece of support for the importance of the environment upon the brain morphology and brain function in humans.

Can the environment influence the human brain and if so,

what type of environment is best? We know from the animal model that environments rich in novelty, socialization opportunity, complexity, and physical activity lead to positive morphological and functional changes in the animal brain. We also have learned that stressful environments can lead to a physiological response of hypersecretion of steroid hormones that destroy hippocampal cells and result in learning deficits across the lifespan. It is from these findings that this book begins to further the discussion of environment on human brain function initiated by Kotulak (1997) and Diamond and Hopson (1998).

Perhaps a unique contribution of this text is a primary focus on health promoting behaviors for the human brain that can be established and encouraged through proper environments and lifestyles. A *lifestyle for brain health and wellness* is derived from the animal and human research on neural plasticity. The description and promotion of a lifestyle for brain health is based on three guiding principles: (1) environment is critical to a developing central nervous system; (2) any environment has some positive and, or negative value upon the developing central nervous system, and (3) the human central nervous system has plasticity and therefore continues to develop and be affected by environment across the lifespan.

Human Environment and Human Brain Development

As with animals, childhood appears to be a critical or highly sensitive time for neuronal development and maturation in the human (Diamond & Hopson, 1998; Kotulak, 1997). Part of the reason for such enormous neuronal development early in life is the fact that the brain has minimal experience and is perhaps hypersensitive to new stimulation. Kotulak (1997) reviewed some of the major early childhood factors thought to promote healthy development of the central nervous system. These include nutrition, intellectual stimulation, empathy, emotional development, language development, mental and physical health, security and safety, trust, and promotion of self-confidence. While these are not meant to be exhaustive, his review of the literature led Kotulak (1997) to emphasize these factors as primary. Clearly, the absence of these factors could be detrimental to a child's developing brain. This was discussed earlier in the book when stress, particularly of a chronic nature, was described as a factor that could compromise neuronal development.

With the early challenge and enrichment from a stimulating environment, there is very little that a young brain cannot accomplish. Our hurried society that forces adults and children to rush from one event to the next, limiting time for a deeper processing of information may in fact run counter to a health promoting environment. Fortunately, we have some control over the type of environment that we expose our children and ourselves. The factors articulated by Kotulak (1997) as important to early development of the central nervous system tend to be the same health promoting factors important across the entire lifespan. As this book argues the importance of a healthy lifestyle for the human brain, the concept of a continuous process of development across the lifespan is required. To this extent, the idea for "sensitive periods" espoused by Thompson and Nelson (2001) rather than age-limited critical periods of neuronal and functional development is supported. The word "period" however should infer life itself and not some limited time within life.

While generalizing concepts from the research on animal brains and environment to humans is an important place to start, specific research that demonstrates a convincing relationship between environment and human brain morphology/function is necessary. Towards this end, a recent study (Moceri, Kukull, Emanuel, Van Belle, & Larson, 2000) found a relationship between early-life childhood and adolescent environment and the risk of AD in late life. According to these authors AD like many other illnesses such as heart disease, stroke, hypertension, and diabetes mellitus may have a link to the early life environment. Interestingly, the areas of the brain affected in AD are the same brain regions that require the most time to mature during childhood and adolescence. These authors argued that a poor-quality childhood or adolescent environment could limit or prevent the brain from maximizing its level of maturation. Two major factors emerged from this community-based-control study to include area of residence before age 18 and number of siblings that related to subsequent development of AD. Specifically, for each additional child in the family the risk of AD increases by 8% and the rural setting, compared to the suburbs, appeared to have a significant relationship to subsequent development of AD. While the idea that larger families may offer increased socialization (positive for brain health) it is important to note that more siblings with fewer resources appears to promote an unenriched environment (negative for brain health).

Interpreting these interesting results requires an understanding of the lessons learned from the early studies on rodents' brain development and environmental enrichment (Diamond & Hopson, 1998). A major lesson from that research was the demonstration of a direct relationship between an enriched environment and brain morphology. The work by Moceri and colleagues (2000) appears to offer a generalization to the human being. The richness and enrichment value of the environment, already demonstrated to have significant value to brain development in animals, appears to have similar import to the development of the human brain. In the study by Moceri and colleagues (2000), an early life environment characterized by poverty may predispose a child to some level of vulnerability to AD in later life.

To explore further the relationship of environment to human brain morphology and function, it is probably wise to refer to the work on environmental enrichment and brain development in animals. This research suggests three factors to be particularly important to making an environment enriched: socialization, mental stimulation, and physical activity. As noted earlier in this text, research on the enriched environment has not advanced to the point of understanding which of these three factors is most important. Regardless, the three factors for environmental enrichment appear useful as an organizational structure for reviewing existing knowledge on the effects of such factors on the human brain.

Socialization

As Diamond and colleagues (1964) published their early work on environmental enrichment and the positive relationship to brain morphology in rodents, socialization (rats in cages with other rats exposed to enriched environments) generated interest as a potentially important factor. Subsequent research has supported a role for socialization (Diamond and colleagues, 1978), and others (Welch, Brown, Welch, & Lin, 1974) have asserted group living for rodents to be a highly significant factor upon brain morphology compared to rodents raised in isolation. Rosenszweig and colleagues (1978) argued that social grouping alone was inadequate to account for the cerebral effects of an enriched environment. The research on socialization and cerebral change in the rodent, therefore, appears to be unresolved. While socialization itself may not account for all of the cerebral change, it does seem to have some import as part of an enriched environment.

The relationship between socialization and cerebral integrity in humans is also inconclusive. To date, however, research suggests a potentially important health role for maintaining high socialization across the lifespan. Katzman (1995) reviewed the idea that what activities a person engages in throughout their life may have an impact upon the integrity of their brain and perhaps affect their vulnerability to neurodegenerative disease. In his editorial review, Katzman cited research (see Fabrigoule et al., 1995) that found a relationship between gardening, knitting, and travel and lowered risk for dementia. Upon closer inspection, these activities appear to load heavily on the neuropsychological variables of planning, visuospatial skill, and novelty. Indeed, with any type of travel, there tends to be a constantly changing environment, rich in novelty and therefore complexity.

This type of natural environment models to some degree the laboratory-based settings described by Diamond and others defined as enriched environments. Much as the cerebral cortex of the rodents responded favorably to such stimulating environments, Katzman may have tapped into the same phenomena with his review of the work on humans. Katzman (1995) was observant to point out that any research that explores the relationship between type of activity and risk of dementia needs to control for education and socioeconomic variables. Further, Katzman pointed out that we do not yet know if a specific set of activities actually limits the risk of dementia or if those with cognitive impairment choose not to engage in certain activities.

More recently, research has explored the relationship between amount of activity, type of activity and risk for dementia. In a study of community dwelling, non-institutionalized elderly, those older persons with five or six social ties were significantly less likely to demonstrate cognitive decline compared to those who had no social ties (Bassuk, Glass, & Berkman, 1999). These authors argued that social engagement, defined as maintaining many social connections with high participation in social activities, may help to prevent cognitive decline in older persons. This relationship held even after controlling for multiple confounds such as age, gender, ethnicity, housing type, education, income, alcohol use, cardiovascular profile, symptoms of depression and level of physical activity.

These authors argued that social engagement challenges persons to communicate effectively and to participate in complex social interactions. Social engagement fosters a dynamic, novel environment for which mobilization is necessary. It also requires a commitment to community and family that may promote purpose and role. Ultimately, social engagement might promote health from contribution and psychological empowerment gained from belonging and self-esteem. There is also an immediate social network fostered by social engagement that can assist in many ways including emotional support.

Even more recently, research has explored the idea that AD may reflect factors or vulnerabilities over the course of a lifetime. In an interesting retrospective study, Friedland and colleagues (2001) analyzed the activity patterns from those suspected of having possible or probable AD compared to controls during their years spanning ages 20 to 60. Using a questionnaire that included 26 non-occupational activities, these authors classified each activity as intellectual, physical, and passive based on diversity and intensity measures. The authors found that the controls were more active during midlife in all three categories compared to the sample with AD, even after controlling for age, education, gender, and income. Interestingly, time devoted to intellectual activities from early adulthood (20-39) to middle adulthood (40-60) was associated with a significant decrease in the risk of AD.

Overall, Friedland and colleagues (2001) concluded that

diversity of activities and intensity of intellectual activities were reduced in the AD sample compared to the control group. Inactivity was proposed as a risk factor for AD and, or as a consequence of early subclinical effects of the disease. Both the review by Katzman (1995) and the research of Friedland and colleagues (2001) indicate a relationship between type and intensity of activity and risk of dementia. This relationship, however, is not causal. Nonetheless, together with the finding for the importance of maintaining **social integration** and reduction of dementia risk (Bassuk et al., 1999), **lifelong activity level** and **social participation** appear to be health-promoting behaviors and critical to a lifestyle for brain health.

Mental Stimulation

Mental stimulation is a general description given to the dynamic interplay between a stimulus and the central nervous system. While our state of the art knowledge is not exact with regard to which activities are more stimulating than others, we have learned that an active mind and body is more healthy than a passive one (Friedland, et al., 2001). Factors critical to increasing the stimulation value of a given stimulus include novelty, complexity, and the presence of other humans. Active engagement of the brain from exposure to new and complicated stimuli therefore appears to have a health promoting value. A reasonable analogy for the health promoting effects of mental stimulation on the brain can be found from the positive effects of an aerobics workout on the cardiovascular system. Our exposure to activities that are mentally stimulating is important, as is the need to identify those environments that facilitate such brain enrichment. Clearly, our school system is an existing vehicle that appears to have inherent value regarding mental stimulation. Indeed, education is one of the sociocultural entities that has been researched with regard to its potential value for brain health.

Education and Brain Health

The finding of a relationship between education and brain development began in the early 1980's (Berkman, 1986; Gurland, 1981) as a result of cross-sectional studies on prevalence rates of AD (Albert, 1995). These early prevalence studies found AD to be significantly more common among those with minimal education compared to those with middle school or more. According to one published report (Beard, Kokmen, Offord, & Kurland, 1992), since 1985 approximately 12 prevalence surveys on AD evaluated sociodemographic factors with only education demonstrating a risk for dementia in older women. These authors reported that in those studies documenting a relationship between low education and risk for AD there was a high rate of illiteracy among those affected by AD (see Pfeffer, Afifi, Chance, 1987). It is important to note that while some studies have argued against a relationship based on methodological concerns (discussed below) (Beard et al., 1992; Bowler, Munoz, Merskey, & Hachinski, 1998; Cobb, Wolf, White, & D'Agostino, 1995), a plethora of research to date makes the relationship between education and risk of dementia difficult to ignore.

The specific methodological concerns raised by the

authors listed above include the need for studies to adequately adjust for age of subjects, consideration for health or medical history such as smoking habits and other potentially deleterious medical risk factors, need to delineate subtypes of dementia with pathological verification, and birth year. Interestingly, while the study by Beard and colleagues (1992) did not find a relationship between low education and risk for AD, the study by Cobb and colleagues (1995) found low educational attainment to be related to increased risk of non-AD dementia (i.e. vascular dementia). It is important to note that the majority of studies reviewed for this book (discussed below) have addressed these methodological concerns in publishing their studies.

On a personal level, I have found some resistance to the idea that education may play a role in limiting or minimizing the risk of dementia and AD in later life. There are multiple reasons for this resistance and it is my opinion that they must be confronted or we run the risk of missing a potentially significant health promoting behavior in our ongoing battle against neurodegeneration. For me, there is nothing sophisticated about the idea that exposing our brain to novel and complex stimuli is healthy. The studies reviewed in this book provide empirical support to this seemingly simple notion. From this context formalized education becomes paramount as the learning that takes place within and across our formalized educational experience in life should be considered a significant example of a complex and novel environment, and therefore health promoting to our brain.

I believe there are two major reasons why resistance to

this idea exists beyond the methodological concerns noted above and generally not reviewed by the lay culture. First our nation's approach and attitude towards health and health promotion is far too medicalized. The grand paradox of our country is that we approach health from a disease perspective. Indeed our very definition of health is absence of disease. As Americans we search for the expensive, invasive, and quick procedure while excluding options that tend to be non-medical, slow to act, and inexpensive. Lifestyle is a primary example of the latter and as Americans we do not give the proper credibility to lifestyle. Despite our lack of appreciation for lifestyle the fact is that a proper lifestyle can enhance longevity and quality of life more than any other single factor. Because of this cultural mindset, we Americans tend not to support the idea that education might be health promoting because it is not medical or even considered a health issue.

Second, we live in a highly politically correct culture reluctant to speak assertively on a given topic for fear of hurting someone or some segment. While it may appear that political correctness is a polite approach it actually can be damaging and cover truths that require serious thought and corrective measures. If education turns out to be a major health promoting "thing" for our brains and overall health we should not let the status-quo of our educational system in this country prevent necessary change. For example, we should not get into discussions about who has opportunities and who does not or develop class, gender, race, or religious division that will distract from the principle that education is health promoting for all humans that have a brain lodged between their ears!

I have experienced both types of resistance when I travel the nation providing workshops on the miracle of the human brain. The point of my workshops and the point of this book are to assert that education must be considered a health promoting experience that potentially has significant value on the integrity of our brains across the lifespan. Given this assertion it is my hope that our nation studies education not only as an academic pursuit (e.g. what age should children learn to read?), but as a health issue (does increased education limit the risk of dementia?). Finally, if education is deemed to have value to the brain as we now accept exercise to have value for our heart the nation must develop more enlightened policies to guarantee that **everyone** is exposed to as much education as he or she desires. Until such a culture shift occurs we must continue to champion non-medical approaches to health and further develop our understanding of how education relates to brain wellness.

To better understand the relationship between enhanced education (number of years in school) and reduced risk of dementia including that caused by AD, a review of the theoretical explanation is needed. The finding of a relationship between education and dementia risk from the early prevalence studies on AD led to a hypothesis that low levels of education may be a risk factor for development of AD or dementia in general (Albert, 1995). One report asserted a biologic effect of education by increasing synaptic density in the brain (Katzman, 1993). By increasing synaptic density early in life it was argued that the brain had a resistance against development of neurodegeneration later in life. Education began to be conceptualized as a vehicle for synaptic growth and therefore as a means of reducing the risk of dementia or of delaying its manifestation. Others have argued for a more general relationship between education and cognitive function rather than specifically to dementia, a finding that appears robust even when studying patients with varying medical illnesses and dementia etiologies (Albert, 1995).

The relationship between education and cognitive change may have several explanations. According to Albert (1995) education may be co-related to or simply facilitate an increase in environmental experiences (recall the enriched environment) that increase cognitive capacity. Those with less education may be exposed to more adverse environments including head injury, poor diet, illness, and poor lifestyles that lead to cognitive change. Such environmental deficiencies have demonstrated negative effects on central nervous system functioning that may increase vulnerability to cognitive decline over time.

A second explanation offered by Albert (1995) is that education may directly affect brain morphology, such as synaptic density as described by the Katzman publication (1993) early in life. Such a physiological function of education on brain integrity is known as "brain reserve" or "intellectual reserve" theory. Intellectual reserve argues that education does not necessarily reduce the risk for disease but rather delays the clinical manifestation of the disease through growth of a more robust brain. In this regard, learning appears to be an important health promoting behavior that contributes to intellectual reserve and a healthier brain. It is important to note that years of school early in life is the typical variable used to operationalize education. However, lifelong learning and lifespan mental stimulation may also be considered important contributors to positive brain development. New learning and new skill acquisition throughout life may also facilitate the effect of education on brain function. The specifics of such new learning are not completely known other than the probable positive effects from novel and complex stimuli.

A final explanation offered by Albert (1995) is that increased levels of education may impact a person's performance on cognitive tests. If an individual begins to experience cognitive decline, their advanced education may provide them with an increased number of problem solving strategies to cope with the decline. The presence of alternative strategies, however, is likely the result of enhanced brain connectivity or synaptic density from increased education. Thus, this explanation has a "chicken or the egg" problem and does not appear to jeopardize the established relationship for education and cognitive function.

Overall, Albert (1995) reasons that our understanding of which explanation is correct will derive from more sophisticated neuroimaging technology that permits direct measurement of brain function and structure. Education appears to have an important relationship to cognitive function despite our inability to explain it. Also, cognitive decline from a variety of medical conditions may be delayed by increased education. An important issue becomes whether education has value only in early life or if it has sustained value across the lifespan.

Further supporting the theoretical and practical import of

intellectual reserve, Mortimer (1997) reviewed prospective clinicopathologic studies and found that a substantial proportion of older, nondemented persons (10% to 67%) demonstrate significant plaques and tangles to meet neuropathologic criteria for AD. Intellectual reserve is used to explain why these individuals do not manifest the disease clinically. Three types of intellectual reserve were presented to include the number of neurons and/or density of their interconnections in childhood; the collection of cognitive strategies for solving problems and taking neuropsychological tests; and the amount of functional brain tissue remaining at any age. Further, Mortimer asserted that intellectual reserve can be promoted by (1) early life nutrition, (2) prevention of cerebrovascular disease, and (3) intellectual stimulation. The idea that early life behavior and lifestyle indirectly serve as important factors to reduce risk of AD was supported.

That education level is related to risk of dementia in late life is generally well established (Jorm, 1997; Stern, Alexander, Prohovnik, & Mayeux, 1992; Stern, Gurland, Tatemichi, Tang, Wilder, & Mayeux, 1994; Schmand et al., 1997; Schmand, Smit, Geerlings, & Lindeboom, 1997). Research indicates that education is not only related to risk of dementia, but that those persons with less than 11 years of education demonstrate earlier and more severe memory decline compared to those with greater than 11 years of school (Schmand et al., 1997).

Exploring the relationship of education level to brain physiology, one study compared three groups of patients with probable AD matched for dementia severity, but with varying educational levels and found cerebral blood flow to be significantly reduced in those patients with the highest level of education (Stern et al., 1992). That is, persons with highest levels of education had more advanced AD though it did not manifest clinically. This finding supports intellectual reserve theory because education may provide a protection against the clinical manifestation of AD even though the neuropathological markers are both present and advanced. Education level itself, therefore is not only related to risk of dementia and cognitive change in later life, it also appears to be a protective factor (Jorm, 1997).

While much of the epidemiological studies cited above have correlated risk of dementia with level of education, another factor relating to dementia risk is occupation that has independent predictive value from education. Using U.S. Census categories for occupation, persons with higher occupational attainment were less likely to manifest dementia (Stern et al., 1994). Higher levels of education and occupational attainment may represent social conduits to intellectual reserve from lifelong mental stimulation and exposure to a relatively enriched environment. Alternatively, higher levels of education and occupational attainment may simply represent expression of innate talents.

An argument for intellectual reserve as the primary explanation for the relationship between lifetime occupational attainment and dementia risk is presented in a study measuring parietal blood flow (Stern et al., 1995). Similar to the cerebral blood flow study described above that found persons with AD and highest levels of education to demonstrate significantly greater cerebral blood flow reductions in parieto-temporal regions, an inverse relationship was found between parietal cerebral blood flow deficits and occupations with higher interpersonal skills and physical demands (Stern et al., 1994). Again, this was true despite the fact that there was no clinical manifestation of the disease. These authors asserted that occupational attainment, independent of education, might provide a reserve that delays the clinical manifestation of AD.

In a subsequent study on education level, occupational attainment and Alzheimer's dementia (Stern, Tang, Denaro, & Mayeux, 1995), clinical expression of AD again was found to be less severe in patients with higher levels of education and occupation. Interestingly, at any level of clinical severity, AD patients with more education and higher occupational attainment were more likely to die soon after clinical diagnosis was rendered. Once again, these results suggest a contributory value of education and occupation to lifelong intellectual reserve that appears to delay the onset of the clinical aspects of AD despite the presence of neuropathological markers. Once the disease manifests clinically, it is already advanced resulting in a relatively short period of time from diagnosis to death.

Still, another study (Evans et al., 1997) assessed the relation of education, occupation (coded on perceived prestige scale), and income to risk of incident clinically diagnosed Alzheimer's disease. Community residents free of AD at baseline and followed on average four years served as subjects. Results from this study indicate all three variables to be related to risk of AD with education demonstrating a stronger relationship than occupation or income. These authors remind us that education and occupation are certainly related to socioeconomic status and that lower socioeconomic status is related to chronic diseases and increased mortality. Whether education, occupation, or income relates to AD because of a general association of poor health or because of a specific disease mechanism is unknown. Regardless, these authors point out that identification of social risk factors for AD not only increases our understanding of the disease, but also provides the opportunity to reverse certain risk factors.

Education Not Related to Dementia Risk

It is important to note that while the majority of studies support a relationship between education and occupation and risk of dementia in late life, other research has argued against such a relationship. For example, one case-control study that used demographic data from an ongoing epidemiological project found no association between AD and education, occupation (U.S. census categories), marital status, or living arrangement (Beard, Kokmen, Offord, & Kurland, 1992). These authors asserted that these variables have minimal value as etiologic risk factors for dementing illness.

Similarly, low educational attainment was found not to be a significant risk factor for the incidence of dementia generally nor AD more specifically (Cobb, Wolf, White, & D' Agostino, 1995). This study focused on incidence of dementia within a community based setting. Utilizing longitudinal methodology and after controlling for age, low educational attainment was associated only with non-AD dementia. The association was thought to be due to deleterious smoking habits and other risk factors for stroke and heart disease.

Finally, multiple demographic and medical variables were studied to determine any relationship with age of onset and rate of progression of AD (Bowler, Munoz, Merskey, & Hachinski, 1998). This retrospective study of data from an ongoing longitudinal project of dementia patients found educational level and occupational level (rating scale of 1 to 3 with 1 being the highest level) not to be related to age of onset or rate of progression of AD. Similarly, there was no relationship found for gender, family history, year of birth, severity of disease, or risk for stroke. Interestingly, birth year had a strong effect on educational level and the occurrence of cerebral infarcts; the earlier the year of birth, the lower the educational level and the greater the risk for stroke. These authors reasoned that birth year must be considered when measuring risk factors for AD. The fact that earlier birth year correlated with lower education and stroke risk likely reflects a generational cohort effect, as fewer educational and health care resources were available for these subjects. Overall, these authors argued against intellectual reserve and against a model of "use it or lose it."

From review of the research above, education and occupation are two more promising components to an emerging lifestyle for a healthy brain. Studies that refute such a relationship are also provided and the methodological concerns of these studies have been reviewed. Such contradictory reports are not uncommon in the medical and social sciences. A critical review of the research suggests there are more than several studies that provide good research, responding to the methodological concerns noted earlier. Given the extensive number of these studies supporting the relationship between education (in particular) and occupation and risk of dementia there is reason to promote these lifestyle opportunities with greater interest. Society provides these two opportunities somewhat naturally as most of us enter school and obtain some form of employment. The critical difference, as proposed by this text, is that education and occupation are not simply things to do as part of life. Rather education and occupation have inherent value for our health, particularly our brain health. From our understanding of intellectual reserve, early and persistent mental stimulation and active engagement in our environment has important health promoting value for our brains! Higher levels of education, lifelong learning and our effort to continuously engage in more complicated and novel tasks within and across occupations are critical components to the healthy brain lifestyle.

Intelligence Versus Education

This chapter has reviewed some of the important research on the relationship between education, occupation, and socioeconomic status and risk for dementia including that caused by AD. These factors or variables are important because they represent environmental conduits to brain stimulation. Each serves to increase the enrichment value of the environment similar to that described within animal research on neurogenesis. Identification of such environmental factors on brain integrity is critical since there is an opportunity to promote those factors that stimulate brain health and to limit those that are deleterious to brain development.

Certainly, education, occupation and other socio-demographic variables may be considered mentally stimulating. The intellectual reserve theory is attractive since it offers one explanation on how such variables might protect the brain from neurodegenerative diseases such as AD. Education and occupational attainment also have import across the lifespan and are not limited by stage of development nor chronological age. There is a natural similarity therefore between the research on environmental enrichment and brain morphology in animals and the benefits of enriched environments for mental stimulation in humans. Closer inspection of this research offers another perspective on the relationship between education, occupation and dementia risk that appeals more to the intrinsic characteristics of the individual.

One important individual characteristic is intelligence as measured by reading capacity or a standard intelligence test. Certainly, it is difficult to differentiate the effects of intelligence from educational attainment, but some have applied statistical models to measure the separate contribution of each on later development of dementia (Plassman, Welsh, Helms, Brandt, Page, & Breitner, 1995). These authors evaluated the relation of education and intelligence in early life to cognitive status in 930 elderly male twins fifty years later. Intelligence, as measured by a standard test of intellect in early adulthood, predicted cognitive status in late life better than educational attainment. Findings suggested that basic cognitive abilities in late life are related to cognitive performance measures from early adult life.

Similarly, both education level and young adult intelligence (intelligence quotient-IQ) are related to cognitive change in elderly persons (Leibovici, Ritchie, Ledesert, & Touchon, 1998). These authors explain, however, that age and cognitive domain are important factors when measuring cognitive change. Age of onset of cognitive change has a strong effect if educational level is low. Young adult IQ appears to exert a protective role in persons older than 75. Education level may have a stronger effect on changes in secondary memory and language functioning while age more strongly predicts cognitive change in areas of new learning.

Premorbid intelligence might reflect intellectual reserve better than educational attainment and therefore might predict dementia more strongly than education level (Schmand, Smit, & Geerlings, 1997). In order to test this hypothesis, 2063 community elderly subjects were tested and followed over four years. Premorbid intelligence was measured using an adult reading test that yields an estimate of verbal intelligence. Results from this study indicate that low premorbid intelligence predicted incident dementia better than low educational level. Interestingly, a high occupational level defined by being in charge of subordinates had a protective effect. The authors assert that these results support intellectual reserve theory and that low premorbid intelligence is an important risk factor for cognitive decline and dementia.

Another study provides support for the importance of early intelligence upon cognitive function in late life (Jorm et al., 1998). Type of occupation was explored to determine if it has any predictive effect on dementia risk or cognitive decline. Data were examined from a longitudinal study of 518 men aged 70 and over. Each participant completed four cognitive tests including an adult reading test, a measure of premorbid intelligence. Occupation for each participant was determined from a standard classification of jobs. Results indicate that occupations to include trade, technical and some service jobs related to poorer cognitive performance and a higher rate of dementia than five other occupational classifications used in the study. The occupational differences on cognitive tests and in dementia prevalence, however, are described as being due to differences in premorbid ability (adult reading test) rather than to differences in rate of cognitive decline. The authors assert support for Mortimer's (1997) work that suggests psychosocial risk factors for dementia may increase one's vulnerability to dementia by reducing the brain's intellectual reserve to a level where even modest pathology results in a dementing process.

More recent research has documented additional support for the importance of childhood mental ability on health in old age. Two hundred eight persons 77 years old from the 1932 Scottish Mental Survey agreed to undergo extensive physical and mental health assessments (Starr, Deary, Lemmon, & Whalley, 2000). Similar to results from other studies, socioeconomic and socioenvironmental factors were found to be important predictors of some physical health problems in late life. However, pre-morbid mental ability assessed in childhood at the age of 11 was found to be an independent predictor of late-life functional independence. As Richards (2000) points out, the study by Starr and colleagues (2000) underscores the enormous influence of childhood experience to health in late life. Richards highlights the study as the first to measure the importance of childhood cognition to health across the lifespan.

Building upon the results published by Starr et al. (2000), Whalley et al. (2000) explored the relationship between childhood mental ability and the presence of dementia using a retrospective data from a 1932 survey of the mental ability of the 1921 Scottish birth cohort. Patients with dementia were located from the 1921 survey and compared to control subjects identified from the 1932 Scottish Mental Survey using the 1932 Moray House Test, a measure of mental ability completed at age 11. Late onset dementia, defined as onset of dementia after 65, was associated with lower mental ability in childhood. Those persons with early onset dementia (dementia onset prior to age 65) did not demonstrate lower childhood mental ability scores compared to controls, nor compared to persons with late-onset dementia. These authors suggest differential biological mechanisms between early onset and late onset dementia. The findings from this study support a link between age-related changes in the central nervous system and onset of dementia in late life. Childhood mental ability appears to modify this link by shaping adult health-related behaviors predisposing to late life dementia. The authors suggest lower childhood mental ability may lead to lower socioeconomic status and behaviors associated with cerebrovascular disease. In contrast, higher childhood mental ability may enable better health information that fosters healthier lifestyle choices. The authors assert that healthy lifestyle choices may reduce exposure to environmental factors associated with cognitive decline.

Towards the issue of intelligence in childhood as health promoting, a recent study (Raine, Reynolds, Venables, & Mednick, 2002) demonstrated that high stimulation seeking three year-old-children scored 12 points higher on total IQ at age 11 compared to low stimulation seekers and also demonstrated higher scholastic and reading ability. This finding represents the first prospective relation between stimulation seeking and intelligence in young children and further supports the power of an enriched environment upon brain and cognitive development. The idea of internal drive to seek or initiate development of an enriched environment is important and deserving of further study. In contrast, it is not known if there are particular reinforcers to initiation of stimulation in the children that could then be replicated. Overall, the importance of cognitive and neuronal development early in life and the relationship of such development upon later intelligence are significant, particularly as it may have longitudinal health promoting effects on the central nervous system.

Intelligence in childhood, measured from a variety of different cognitive tests, therefore appears to have fundamental import regarding functional status and dementia risk manifested clinically later in life. Intelligence also may be an independent and perhaps more significant component to health in later life than education level. Further, intelligence in childhood appears to relate to occupational status, socioeconomic potential, and a variety of lifestyle factors that might support or counter an enriched environment. There also appears to be a positive effect of self-initiation of stimulation seeking behavior in the creation of an enriched environment. From this perspective, **intelligence in childhood** becomes an important factor of the lifestyle for a healthy brain.

Is Dementia a Childhood Problem?

How extreme is the idea that AD is a childhood problem? Perhaps not as extreme as it sounds. In addition to studies reviewed above that demonstrated the importance of intelligence at age 11 upon risk of dementia after age 65 (Starr et al., 2000; Whalley, et al. 2000), one study found an association between an adverse environment in childhood and AD (Moceri, Kukull, Emanuel, van Belle, & Larson, 2000). These authors point out a relationship already exists between chronic diseases such as heart disease, stroke, hypertension, and diabetes and early life environment. Further, these authors note that those areas of the brain most vulnerable to AD are the identical areas of the brain that take the longest to mature during childhood and adolescence. A poor quality childhood or adolescent environment therefore might be detrimental to development of these critical brain regions leading to an increased vulnerability to AD or other neurodegenerative diseases. Interestingly, these authors found area of residence before age 18 and number of siblings to be associated with development of AD later in life. More controls than cases grew up in suburbs and for each additional sibling, the risk of AD increased by 8%. The presence of APOE4 (specific risk marker on the blood protein apolipoprotein) and education level did not modify the relationship. The authors concluded that early-life childhood and adolescent environment is related to risk of AD.

Early Childhood Environment and Dementia

The early chapters of this book reviewed the research on environmental enrichment and brain morphology in animals. Environments rich in mental stimulation, socialization, and physical activity characterized enrichment and promoted rodent neurogenesis in the dentate gyrus of the hippocampus. Such neurogenesis occurred in other animals including non-human primates into adulthood. While such research has been the focus of intense attention and some scrutiny (Rakic, 2002), there is little doubt regarding the relationship between environment and brain development.

This animal model is appealing to investigation of environmental effects upon human childhood development, particularly within the central nervous system. Similar to animals, an environment that deprives children and their brains of mental stimulation can be detrimental by increasing the vulnerability of the brain to dementia (Kotulak, 1997; Moceri et al., 2000; Whalley et al. 2000). Environmental enrichment therefore also appears to have some credibility for the developing human brain and may continue to be important across the lifespan (Snowdon, 2001; Whalley, 2001). Certainly, there are examples of factors such as head injury (Plassman et al., 2000), poverty (Moceri et al., 2000), and chronic stress (Sapolsky, 1996;

Sapolsky, 1998) that may increase the risk for dementia in later life. While such risk factors are important to identify, the prevention of such factors in one's life is likely more important. Such prevention represents an effort towards a proactive lifestyle of health promotion for the developing human brain.

Health Promoting Behaviors for the Brain

We have learned a great deal over the past 50 years regarding the contributions our lifestyle might have upon the health of our hearts and entire body. We know for example that a lifestyle of exercise, proper diet, proper weight, refrain from excessive alcohol consumption and not smoking increases the chance for longevity and health of the heart. Most importantly, health care policy has applied this understanding to practical recommendations and incentives for maintaining a lifestyle for healthy hearts. As a result, while heart disease remains the primary cause of death in the United States, the rate of deaths due to cardiac disease has not increased.

A similar understanding is needed for the health of the human brain. This text has reviewed the important factors necessary for enrichment of the environment in animals. The finding that enriched environments promote brain development in animals requires closer attention for its similar effect upon the human brain. Likewise environments with little or no stimulation, few resources, and general deprivation have demonstrated negative effects on the brain (Moceri et al., 2000; Sapolsky, 1996; Sapolsky, 1998). Building our understanding of the proper environments and input to our brains for preventing or delaying the onset of neurodegeneration can lead to a defined lifestyle for brain health and wellness. There is no reason the nation cannot adopt health policy that champions healthy lifestyles for healthy brains!

This text has highlighted several of the components of a healthy lifestyle and enriched environment for the brain. These components include **socialization, activity** and limiting passivity in early adulthood (Bassuk et al., 1999; Fabrigoule et al., 1995; Friedland et al., 2001; Katzman, 1995; Snowdon, 2001), **higher levels of education** defined by more years of school (Albert, 1995; Stern et al., 1994), **higher levels of occupation** (Jorm et al., 1998; Stern et al., 1994), and **higher intelligence quotients** in **early life** (Plassman et al., 1995; Schmand et al., 1997). Similarly, low socioeconomic status (Evans et al., 1997; Moceri et al., 2000), presence of chronic stress (Lemaire et al., 2000; Sapolsky, 1996; Sapolsky, 1998; Smith, 1996), and head injury in childhood and early adult years (Plassman et al., 2000) represent components to a lifestyle that may increase the risk for AD and related dementias in late life.

The Significance of Learning

Another important component to a lifestyle for a healthy human brain is **learning**. A strong predictor of sustained mental function in late life was education (Rowe and Kahn, 1998) suggesting early childhood education is critical to brain development and lifelong learning is important for mental stimulation across the lifespan. Acquiring knowledge is not only a neurophysiological event it may also represent a health promoting behavior necessary for development and growth of the central nervous system. Research from the animal model indicates that learning is related to neurogenesis (Gould, et al., 1999A; Kempermann & Gage, 1999) and that this effect continues through adult years (Gould, et al., 1999B). Importantly, neurogenesis occurs in the hippocampus of young and adult rodents and non-human primates, the brain region most important for learning. Why neurogenesis occurs in this brain region is not completely understood. It is reasonable to speculate, however, that the anatomy necessary for learning should have the capacity to develop new brain cells and to have a capacity to respond to environmental input. The central nervous system is primarily an information processor. The brain needs to process information and therefore benefits from a capacity to maintain a healthy hippocampus throughout life. Such reasoning is derived from a Darwinian perspective. Alzheimer's disease is one example of a leading cause of progressive dementia in humans that destroys the hippocampus and learning ability early in the disease process.

For humans, learning is critical for advancing the human condition in general. With learning new ideas and methods for enhancing our general well being emerge. The importance of learning, therefore, cannot be overstated. Whether or not neurogenesis has been confirmed in humans does not detract from the importance of learning in humans. Supporting similar capacity of plasticity in humans to that of animals, recent research suggests that the human central nervous system continues to develop into adulthood (Bartzokis et al., 2001; Giedd et al., 1999; Sowell et al., 1999). Neurogenesis in the human brain has also been established in two studies (Eriksson et al., 1998; Roy et al., 2000). Perhaps most importantly, human neurogenesis reportedly occurs in the dentate gyrus of the hippocampus, an area critical for new learning and the same region where neurogenesis occurs in animals.

These recent studies use more advanced technologies and may simply reflect our advancement in measuring what has always existed. Plasticity and neurogenesis as one form of human brain plasticity is critical for it permits the possibility for the positive effects of environmental enrichment across the lifespan. As part of this text's specific premise that a lifestyle for a healthy brain can be developed and followed, research on learning as part of this lifestyle for brain health is reviewed.

Clearly, the studies reviewed above lay a foundation for the idea that a more educated and intellectually stimulated brain, defined by the number of years of formalized school, and elevated scores on measures of intellect, yields some protection against neurodegeneration. While there is no consensus whether education itself or the intelligence derived from such educational exposure is the primary factor in limiting dementia, there is little doubt that early and lifelong mental stimulation is critical. Beyond education that is a broad based vehicle for learning, more specific types of learning may contribute to brain health. Language acumen has attracted significant interest not only regarding human brain development, but also within studies of AD.

Language as One Type of Learning

There is little doubt that humans have a highly developed

sophisticated language capacity unlike most other animals. The reason for such complexity is not entirely known though our language skills have enabled human beings to develop in significantly advanced ways. Interestingly, the vast majority of humans have language designated primarily in the left-hemisphere of the brain, a primary reason why the hemisphere where language resides is labeled "dominant." Similar to our lack of understanding as to why our language system is so advanced, we do not yet know why language is primarily a left-hemisphere function (Collins, 2001). The human brain appears to need language as evidenced by the brain's ability in newborns to shift language to the right hemisphere when the left hemisphere is missing.

The exact reason for language, the neural systems underlying language, and the potential relationship of language to health are fundamental concerns. Language development has enormous significance for an individual's capacity for learning, education, occupation, intelligence, and socioeconomic status. In this regard, it is reasonable to consider language development and development of a robust language system as health promoting. Regarding language and its potential role for brain health, several different lines of research have contributed to the articulation of such a relationship.

Language and Alzheimer's Disease

David Snowdon is an epidemiologist who has generated much insight regarding Alzheimer's disease from his longitudinal investigation of nuns known as the "Nun Study" (Snowdon, 2001). As an epidemiologist, Snowdon has the great fortune of having access to a relatively homogeneous population (nuns) who not only have maintained life records, but who have volunteered their brains for study at the time of death. These aspects of his investigation are universally unique. The careful inspection of the nun's medical and psychosocial records from early in life can be combined with precise neuroanatomical measurements of their brains at autopsy.

One of the major findings of his work, summarized in his text (Snowdon, 2001) is that nuns tend to suffer AD at a rate less than the general population. While the definitive reason for this finding may not yet be known, Snowdon and his colleagues underscore the importance of mental stimulation and lifelong learning, diet, and prayer. Nuns without AD tend to demonstrate a rigorous lifestyle filled with mental stimulation and intellectual enrichment. To this extent, the behavior of these fortunate nuns fits nicely with what is expected from the intellectual reserve theory and the "use it or lose it" model of brain health.

Perhaps of equal or more significance is the work that Snowdon and colleagues (Snowdon et al., 1996) have published on early language skills and prediction of late life neurodegeneration. Linguistic ability was assessed in ninety-three nuns from inspection of their autobiographies written when the ladies were on average 22 years of age. Linguistic ability was defined by two variables: (1) idea density, defined as the average number of ideas expressed per ten words and (2) grammar complexity, rated on a zero (simple sentence) to seven (complex sentence) scale. For each of the ninety-three nuns, cognitive function was also assessed in late life (average of 58 years later) using a battery of tests.

For each nun in the study who died, neuropathologic analysis was conducted on the brain for confirmation of AD that included presence of neurofibrillary tangles (entanglement of fibril substance detected under the microscope thought to be a neuropathologic marker of AD). Results indicate young ladies whose autobiographies were rated for low idea density at approximately the age of 22 also demonstrated substantially more neurofibrillary tangles in their hippocampi and neocortex (region of the cortex to develop most recently) at the time of death compared to those with high idea density in their autobiographies. Grammar complexity in early life did not provide as strong a relationship to neuropathologically confirmed AD at autopsy.

Snowdon et al., (1996) suggest low linguistic ability in early life represents a strong marker for cognitive impairment and neuropathological changes of AD in late life. Alternatively, highly developed linguistic ability in early adulthood might represent healthy brains more resistant to the pathologic changes of AD in late life. It is unknown whether linguistic ability represents an early risk factor for a brain vulnerable to AD in later life, or if the neuropathology of AD has already begun to manifest in early adulthood in the form of reduced language capacity. Regardless, this study, similar to others noted above (Reiman et al., 1996; Reiman et al., 1998) support the idea that AD and perhaps other forms of dementia begin to manifest much earlier in life than previously thought.

Implications for Early Language Acquisition

The idea proposed by Snowdon et al., (1996) that linguistic ability in early life may have a protective role against neurodegeneration in late life offers additional support to the idea for a proactive lifestyle for brain health. Clearly, language development is a highly complex and specialized area of research beyond the scope of this text. However, language development may occur at the earliest of ages (Goodwyn, Acredolo, & Brown, 2000). It is also generally known that those with advanced language systems tend to perform better in school, have higher intelligence, more occupational opportunities, and higher socioeconomic status in life. Each of these factors has been discussed in this and other texts as important to our general and cognitive health. Language itself, therefore, may be a catalyst for the enriched environments our brains need to thrive throughout life. If this is true, it is critically important that we implement methods to develop the language system as early as possible. Indeed, perhaps more critical to the discussion of language development and its potential protective role against AD and late life neurodegeneration is how soon can the human brain begin to develop language?

This is not an easy question to answer because language may take multiple forms (Goodwyn, Acredolo, & Brown, 2000). For example, oral language tends to develop around the first year of life. However, prior to oral language, babies respond to their environments including their mother's voice, prosody of spoken language, to faces, and to stressful input. Additionally, symbolic gesturing is a form of language that may begin around 10 months of age. Significant to the discussion of language development at the earliest of age, Goodwyn and colleagues (2000) assert that symbolic gestures represent a critical step in symbolic development and facilitate communication development in babies and children.

Development of oral language and the neural systems that underlie it appears to be critical if linguistic acumen has a health-promoting role for our brains. As noted earlier, most humans have expressive and comprehension language distributed across a neural network within the dominant left hemisphere. More specifically, Broca's region located in the posterior left frontal lobe is thought to facilitate speech while Wernicke's region located in the left superior temporal lobe subserves comprehension. The arcuate fasiculus is a band of white matter that connects Broca's region to Wernicke's area thereby permitting repetition of words and sounds. The development and nurturing of this critical neural system underlying language would seem to be important.

While reading to children, playing music to children, and encouraging speech output regardless of its developmental maturity have all been encouraged, other research might point to a more empirically based methodology for earliest development of the language system. Symbolic gesturing is a form of language that has demonstrated benefit on early language development (Goodwyn, Acredolo, & Brown, 2000). According to their early work (Acredolo & Goodwyn, 1985) gestures such as an adult holding out his or her hands to a contemplating baby represents a form of communication even when oral communication is not present. Symbolic representation is found in both hearing and deaf children and it has import for it represents a foundation for representational behavior in multiple domains including language. Indeed, symbolic gesturing may represent the early stage of oral communication.

Using a case study, Acredolo & Goodwyn (1985) taught a hearing baby informal signs as a means of nonverbal labeling and communication. By the age of 17.5 months, the young female learned 29 signs and she had an oral vocabulary that reached 109 words. For this case, the authors indicate that the child's rate of vocal development was considerably faster than age appropriate normative data. Further, symbolic signs were argued to be part of early language development.

In a subsequent study on symbolic gesturing in normal infants as young as 11 months gestural labels was found again to be positively related to verbal vocabulary development (Acredolo & Goodwyn, 1988). These authors assert that gestural language develops in tandem with children's early expression of words, but that eventually, oral language dominates communication replacing gestural or symbolic expression.

Perhaps most interesting for purposes of this text is the study of the long-term impact of symbolic gesturing during infancy on Intelligence Quotient (IQ) at age 8 (Acredolo & Goodwyn, 2000). This longitudinal study explored the impact of active symbolic gesturing taught to infants by their parents upon intellect as measured by standardized testing post 2nd grade. Compared to controls, infants taught sign language that relied on symbolic gestures scored significantly higher on a standardized test of intelligence at 8 years of age (post-2nd grade). The authors speculated that both cognitive and socio-emotional factors contributed to the significant differences found on IQ. Positive effects of early symbolic gesturing on verbal development were thought to provide a cognitive boost for expressive and receptive language relative to controls. Symbolic gesturing may also have enabled infants and children to seek and acquire more information about topics on their own leading to increased general knowledge. Infants trained with symbolic gesturing were also found to have high self-confidence and positive interactions with adults, factors that likely contribute to enhanced intelligence. Interestingly, parents and other adults were found to have a positive attitude towards the abilities of children trained with symbolic gesturing. Overall, these authors underscore their findings that symbolic gesturing taught to toddlers increased IQ several years later, and enriched the interpersonal lives between toddlers and significant others in their environment.

Fundamental to the issue of oral versus gestural language development is the study of neural systems underlying each. As noted above, language that relies on speech output and comprehension of oral language utilizes the left hemisphere primarily. What are less widely studied are the neural systems underlying gestural or more motor-based language. One example of such non-speech based language with linguistic structure is sign language. American Sign Language (ASL) is a language that is not speech-based yet possesses phonological, morphological, and syntactic levels of language organization nearly identical to those of spoken language. Further, ASL relays full semantic and grammatical expression and employs similar rules of conversation to spoken languages.

Using positron emission tomography (PET) technology with profoundly deaf subjects, Petito and colleagues (2000) found cerebral blood flow during signing in areas of the brain that are nearly identical to hearing persons, a finding supported by other research (Bellugi, 1994). These results suggest that specific sites of the left frontal cortex are involved in higher order linguistic processing and do not depend on the presence of sound. This work which finds similar if not identical neural systems of language in the hearing and deaf likely explains the results of Acredolo and colleagues (2000) above who documented enhanced intelligence in toddlers taught symbolic gesturing or sign. Further study of persons profoundly deaf might help to better explain the neural basis of language.

Further supporting the need of the infant to develop language, itself a fundamental need of the central nervous system, is a study on babbling of hearing babies born to deaf parents (Petito, Holowka, Sergio, & Ostry, 2001). According to these authors, healthy infants begin to babble around 7 months of age. It is thought that this babbling represents the origins of language development. Hand movements were studied in hearing babies born to profoundly deaf parents to determine if any pattern existed to help better understand babbling. Petito and colleagues (2001) found hearing babies born to profoundly deaf parents produce hand activity distinct from other uses of their hands. Further the hand movements contain specific rhythmic patterns of natural language thought to represent silent babbling. These authors assert that babies are sensitive to rhythmic language patterns and this sensitivity is critical to launching the process of language acquisition.

To summarize, language is an important aspect of learning and is thought to be necessary and fundamental to the human being. There appears to be a common neural system underlying language in the human brain. This neural system is nearly identical if not identical in the brains of humans with hearing to those who are deaf. Language itself, therefore, may not require sound. Toddlers have both the need and the capacity to communicate prior to oral language. Such communication occurs naturally in the form of symbolic gestures. There is both an expressive and receptive gestural capacity in toddlers. Toddlers taught sign language via gestures develop self-confidence and positive interpersonal relations with parents and significant others in their environments. Further, these toddlers have higher IQs several years later when they graduate from the second grade. **Gestural language** therefore is proposed as one method to develop the language system prior to initiation of oral language.

If gestural language taught to toddlers increases their language skills and intelligence longitudinally, gestural communication might be considered a methodology or a practical tool for fighting neurodegeneration in late life. Research presented in this text indicates that more sophisticated linguistic acumen relates to fewer neurofibrillary tangles in the brains at time of death. Additionally, higher IQ early in life also relates to a lower risk of dementia in late life. As a more developed language system also relates to higher IQ, these correlational findings support the proactive development of our language system early in life, prior to onset of oral language. Gestural communication at the earliest age provides one tool to nurture the neural network underlying language in the human brain and it appears not to matter if the person is hearing or deaf.

Physical Exercise

There is no doubt that physical exercise increases cardiovascular health. The research on the physical and psychological benefits of exercise has been well documented and certainly extends beyond the scope of this book. Perhaps Rowe and Kahn (1998) established the benefit of exercise on human health most succinctly by asserting that fitness reduces your risk of dying. Exercise and physical activity has important contributions to brain health as established in the animal model where a direct relationship is established between physical exercise and brain morphology.

Running in a wheel increases neurogenesis in the adult mouse dentate gyrus, a brain structure critical for memory and new learning (Van Praag, Kempermann, & Gage, 1999). Running has also increased synaptic plasticity and learning in adult mice (Van Praag, Christie, Senjnowski, & Gage, 1999). These two studies support the idea that physical activity has an important role in hippocampal neurogenesis and learning.

For humans, it has been known for a long time that physical exercise in moderation relates to enhanced cardiac health, improved sense of well being, increased energy, improved cognition, and improved sleep. The significant interaction between the cardiovascular system and the central nervous system is also well established (Angevine & Cottman, 1981). The brain utilizes nearly 25% of the blood volume from each heartbeat. For a system that weighs only two to four pounds at maturity, the amount of energy the brain requires is staggering. Practically, there is an awakened understanding of the importance of the relationship between the heart and the brain. Our lifestyles that enhance the health of the heart through diet, exercise, stress reduction, meditation and prayer, reduction of smoking, reducing obesity and treating hypertension also enhance the health of the brain.

Consideration for the critical relationship between cerebrovascular disease and AD is offered by Snowdon (2001). He speculates that the presence of cerebrovascular disease is necessary to essentially trigger the plaques and tangles within the brains of those with AD. It is unclear if AD is expressed without the presence of the cerebrovascular disease. Snowdon's thoughts reflect the fact that some of the brains of the nuns in his longitudinal study have sufficient plaques and tangles in their brains at the time of death to render the diagnosis of AD yet they never manifested the disease clinically in life.

Clearly, the importance of physical activity upon the central nervous system is also reflected in research that demonstrates an inverse relationship between passivity (Friedland et al., 2001) and social isolation (Bassuk et al., 1999) in middle adulthood and risk of dementia in late life. These studies encourage a physically active life with social participation across the lifespan. Our ability to avoid passivity and social isolation throughout life, therefore, promotes the health of our central nervous system. The relationship between passivity and poor health in later life is also supported by the MacArthur Foundation Study on Successful Aging (Rowe & Kahn, 1998). This study examined a representative sample of 4,000 older Americans from the eastern United States and found frailty in older age may be reversible with aerobic exercise and weight training. Fitness in older adults was noted to increase significantly with walking several days a week for forty-five minutes per day. Weight training also enhanced physical fitness in older persons, increased muscle strength, and reduced weight.

Physical fitness not only increases health of older persons but also reduces the risk of specific illnesses of later life. According to Rowe and Kahn (1998) physical activity reduces the risk of coronary heart disease by as much as 80% compared to passive persons. Physical activity and achieving physical fitness also has benefit in reducing the risk of high blood pressure, colon cancer, diabetes, arthritis, osteoporosis, balance problems, and falls. Dance and Tai Chi have been found to be useful activities for balance and reduction of falls.

Despite the significant value of physical exercise and fitness on health in the older person, Rowe and Kahn (1998) found the average older person is not vigorous and does not participate in regular physical activity. Passivity appears to increase with advanced age: 33% of women and 25% of men between ages 65 and 74 do not participate in any leisure time physical activities. Further, 50% of women and 40% of men over the age of 75 do not participate in regular physical activity.

Overall, only 20% of the older age group may participate in regular exercise, despite being more vulnerable to illness and frailty than younger persons.

The MacArthur Foundation Study of Successful Aging (Rowe & Kahn, 1998) found a relationship between higher mental function in late life and preserved physical function. It is known that one of the primary concerns of older persons is loss of mental function and loss of independence. Preservation of independence therefore is a clear motivating factor for older persons to remain physically active and can be reinforced to adopt a lifestyle that promotes mental health. Rowe and Kahn (1998) also found that physical exercise leads to enhanced cognitive function, particularly memory, by increasing nerve growth factor, which in turn may promote neuron development. This idea is derived from research demonstrating such an effect of exercise on nerve growth factor in the brains of adult rats.

Recent research further supports the idea that physical exercise protects brain function in rats (Cotman & Engesser-Cesar, 2002). Rats who participated in voluntary wheel running demonstrated greater brain-derived neurotrophic factor that support the functions of cognition, sensation, and motor functions. These authors argue that exercise not only improves cognitive functioning but may also enhance the plasticity of the brain. Such plasticity might reduce the negative consequences of brain damage and delay the onset of neurodegenerative disease.

The benefit of exercise and physical activity to animals and humans is generally accepted. The studies cited above reflect the multifaceted contributions of physical activity to the overall health of the human. For purposes of this book, studies that document a relationship between physical activity and brain health promotion have been reviewed. Healthy samples are typically studied and physical activity is found to promote health and delay onset of cognitive decline. However, exercise has also been found to be a positive behavior for those persons already suffering dementia (Arkin, 1999). A relatively small sample of older persons diagnosed with mild to moderately severe dementia of the Alzheimer's type demonstrated physical and emotional benefit from a regular supervised exercise program including aerobics and weight training.

In a subsequent prospective study of the same sample (Arkin, 2001) cognitive deterioration was slowed in the sample of patients with AD compared to matched controls. Again, physical exercise including weight training and aerobic exercise over a 28-week period of time provided benefit to slowing a neurodegenerative process (Arkin, 2001). The author indicates the need to delineate the contribution of the exercise component to overall slowing of the dementing process from other potential factors such as cognitive stimulation and socialization throughout the 28-week program. This study, however, provides important insight to the potential therapeutic intervention of physical exercise within an enriched environment for persons diagnosed with AD.

The critical point for purposes of this text is that physical activity, social engagement, and active contribution (expressing oneself versus passively listening) throughout the lifespan appears to have import for brain health. The manner in which our nation applies such knowledge to a lifestyle similar to that dedicated to cardiac health remains unknown. The purpose of this text is to underscore the importance and need of a strong commitment to brain health not unlike that already applied for the heart. The delineation of a lifestyle for a healthy brain is presented in the next chapter.

Chapter Six
Lifestyle for a Healthy Brain

This final chapter proposes a proactive lifestyle as important to brain health across the lifespan. The lifestyle for brain health is built from our understanding of environment and brain in the animal that was reviewed earlier in this book. It is important to note that while a proactive lifestyle requires individual responsibility and personal change there also is a need for a significant cultural shift regarding "health care" in order for there to be true commitment to lifestyle as a health promoting force. At present, our culture remains highly medicalized, invasive and impatient. Change from this approach will require time and persistence. This book represents part of an ongoing effort to prioritize the brain as a critical part of our being and to elevate those lifestyle behaviors that maximize its capacity and sustain its health. The chapter begins by articulating a conceptual and theoretical basis for a lifestyle towards brain health. Then ideas for cultural change are provided that foster a proper setting for development and implementation of a lifestyle for brain health. Finally, the specifics and practice of a proactive and lifelong lifestyle for brain health are presented.

Conceptual Foundation

The concept of a proactive comprehensive lifestyle for a healthy human brain represents a unique offering of this book. Indeed this text encourages a national commitment to an applied practice of brain health to model that already established for our cardiac system. Consider how our nation has taken important findings from the clinical science of cardiology and applied them to a behavioral practice for all to follow. We have aerobic centers and gymnasiums with membership costs that may be partially reimbursed by health insurance companies. Exercise rooms and swimming pools are in nearly every hotel in the nation and some airports also provide exercise facilities. Exercise shows are now a standard part of early morning television programming. Restaurants have special sections of the menu for foods that promote a healthy heart. Similarly, grocery stores have special aisles filled with foods promoting a healthy heart. Dr. Ornish (Ornish, 1990) has demonstrated the health promoting utility of diet and lifestyle for those with cardiac illness. These are but a few of the examples of how our nation has applied research findings to promote a healthier heart and healthier human being.

Interestingly our society has also demonstrated an entrenched acceptance of the heart as a system that defines us. Daily phrases such as "I love you with all my heart," "you broke my heart," and "the team played their hearts out," suggest such an acceptance or level of comfort. When providing workshops on the human brain I often have fun by reminding the audience that the heart also has been given its own holiday, Valentine's Day! Using the metaphor of the Wizard of OZ, this text seeks not to push the "Tin Man" who was searching for his heart off the stage, but rather to the side. Our nation can now benefit from directing attention and resources towards the "Scarecrow" who was searching for a brain. By casting energies toward brain health our nation can prioritize the importance of the central nervous system and promote a proactive lifestyle that develops healthy brains resistant to neurodegenerative disorders of late life.

Leading scientists and authors (Diamond & Hopson, 1998; Kotulak, 1997; Snowdon, 2001) have made suggestions and direct recommendations for enhancing mental stimulation or building a more enriched environment for children. This text builds upon these recommendations by initiating a process towards articulation of a nationally supported lifestyle for a healthy brain. The animal research clearly establishes a relationship between environment and morphological change in the brain. To the extent that the human brain has similar capacities as those of the animal brain, it is worthwhile to direct our attention to those factors most critical for neurogenesis in the animal. It is from these factors that a lifestyle for a healthy human brain can be articulated.

Clearly, there has not been enough research to establish convincingly neurogenesis in the human brain. Indeed, the academic tension regarding neurogenesis within animal research itself remains strong (Rakic, 2002). Nonetheless, recent research (Eriksson et al., 1998) suggests human neurogenesis in the hippocampal structures, the same region where neurogenesis occurs in animals. Additional research in the animal (Bjornson, Rietze, Reynolds, Magli, & Vescovi, 1999) and human (Giedd et al., 1999) amplify the reality of neural plasticity and open the door for more creative concepts towards brain health.

Further supporting a need to think and act more proactively towards health of the human brain is the fact that AD and other neurodegenerative disorders will increase with the burgeoning number of older Americans. Also, while science may find a cure for AD in our lifetime, there are only four cognitive enhancing medications in use today approved by the Food and Drug Administration. All four are effective somewhat in slowing the course of AD if given to patients in the early stages of the disorder. Our long-term care option is expensive and significantly unpopular and our Medicare system lacks a clear understanding of how to care for older Americans. From this context it is relatively simple to understand the need for increased attention towards health of the central nervous system, for a well-articulated lifestyle that guides consumers towards brain health, and for a health promotion system that champions a lifestyle for health across the lifespan.

Theoretical Foundation

There is research to justify a strategic initiative towards brain health in the United States of America. Though most studies are correlational there appears to be a robust relationship between mental stimulation, education level, occupation level, socialization, physical activity and increased cognitive capacity and reduced risk of neurodegenerative disease. Research also indicates that language sophistication and intelligence early in life correlates with reduced risk of dementia and cognitive deficits in later life. In contrast, poverty and stress can delay and retard central nervous system development perhaps increasing vulnerability to neurodegenerative disease with advanced age. Taking these findings and applying them to practice both behaviorally and with health care policy is needed!

One theoretical construct that helps to explain the health promoting value of these psychosocial factors is intellectual reserve also referred to as brain reserve. As reviewed earlier in this book, intellectual reserve refers to the neurophysiological development of the central nervous system via mental stimulation across the lifespan. The theory espouses that with increased challenge and new learning the brain reacts by literally developing more synaptic density (greater number of connections between neurons) and greater cortical volume thereby offering a defense against degenerative diseases. It may also be that with increased intellectual reserve we delay the time before a disease clinically manifests. Whether intellectual reserve prevents clinical manifestation of disease or delays its onset the importance of developing a robust brain through increased synaptic density across the lifespan is supported.

Returning to the animal research on brain development and neurogenesis, three factors were defined as critical to an enriched environment: (1) mental stimulation, (2) socialization, and (3) physical activity. These factors were reviewed earlier and are argued to be as equally important to the health of the human brain. In addition to these three factors, it is proposed that any environment deemed enriched for the human brain will include *complexity* and *novelty*. For each stimulus processed by our human brain the degree to which it is promoting our intellectual reserve is likely based upon how complex and novel the stimulus is. This may always be defined somewhat on an individual basis given a person's history (i.e., piano playing versus hitting a baseball), though some stimuli will have universal complexity and novelty (i.e., advanced math). It is argued that those stimuli rich in novelty and complexity will promote intellectual reserve more successfully than stimuli characterized as rote and passive. It is further argued that the higher cortical structures of the brain are stimulated more with an environment rich in novelty and complexity while environments that are rote and passive do not engage the cortex in the same manner. Finally, it is interesting to note that as we persist in activities that are complex and novel these same activities will become rote and passive for us. Such transition from the novel and complex to the rote and passive has a neurophysiological basis likely reflecting increased synaptic reserve. The phrase "practice makes perfect" takes on a whole new meaning!

Intellectual reserve suggests two critical assumptions important to the discussion of a proactive lifestyle for healthy brains. First, each person has some control regarding his or her lifestyle towards brain health. Second, intellectual reserve does not appear to be limited or fixed at any one age. Indeed, the capacity of the human central nervous system may be bound only by life itself. It is from these two assumptions, borne from intellectual reserve theory, that a proactive lifestyle for a healthy human brain is based.

Fundamentally, therefore, all environmental input to the brain can be framed from a health perspective with the goal being to increase the amount of time our brains are exposed to highly stimulating, enriched (complex and novel), and health promoting environments. It is from such exposure that intellectual reserve-synaptic density is most likely to develop and expand.

Any lifestyle promoting brain health must be considered a lifelong continuous process distinct from our current approach that artificially frames stages of the lifespan. This book argues that the primary neurodegenerative diseases of late life are actually triggered much earlier in life and perhaps may be better conceptualized as *childhood disorders*. Such a concept has support from studies that demonstrate AD to evince neurophysiological degenerative effects significantly before clinical manifestation of the disease (Reiman et al. 1996) and from the relationship between poverty in childhood and increased risk of AD in late life (Moceri et al. 2000). If neurodegenerative diseases that manifest clinically in late life actually develop in early childhood the idea of a proactive and lifelong lifestyle for brain health is underscored.

Need for A Cultural Shift

The United States employs a highly medicalized approach to health. There is an over reliance on procedures that are invasive, expensive, and quick. Americans demand a rapid fix to their problems that is underscored by our nation's significantly high utilization of medications even in childhood. Our approach to health is certainly reactive and more disease driven than health promoting. We have primitive ideas regarding wellness and health is typically defined as absence of disease. There is presently no financial incentive to engage in a lifestyle that will help to resist disease. From this rather entrenched and traditional context, change in social policy will not be easy.

A nation interested in health promotion of the central nervous system will recognize the importance of a proactive and lifelong lifestyle. Similarly, it is important to underscore the importance of health promotion rather than disease treatment alone. In this regard, lifestyle and health promotion become proactive issues worthy of the same place within any health insurance plan as more invasive, reactive procedures. Today we typically refer to such non-medicalized approaches as "alternative" that carries a subtle tone of being less useful. Change at the societal and policy level requires a significant reconceptualization of health and those behaviors that promote health across the lifespan. As research continues to demonstrate the health promoting benefits of particular behaviors a lifestyle can be articulated and reinforced financially and socially.

For real cultural change it is necessary to first educate Americans about how the human brain operates and second what the brain needs in order to develop in a healthy manner. As Americans learn about their brain and those behaviors that maximize its health they will have an opportunity to change their own behavior in positive ways. While there is no guarantee that education alone leads to behavior change, identifying specific behaviors that promote brain health will empower the individual to take control of their brain health.

A lifelong continuous model of brain enrichment necessitates a health promoting lifestyle that is equally life-long. This chapter articulates a lifestyle for the human brain based on a lifelong continuous model of neural plasticity. It is argued that brain enrichment from the earliest stages of life and across the entire lifespan will maximize the health of the human brain, increase intellectual reserve, and increase the brain's ability to fight off or delay the clinical manifestation of neurodegeneration later in life. While this book does not presume a specific formulary, there is enough information to forward a general lifestyle for brain health promotion. In articulating such a lifestyle for the healthy brain, we can rely on the three major factors found to enrich the brain in animals: *mental stimulation, physical activity, and socialization* while emphasizing the importance of the *complex and novel.* To not support such a proactive lifestyle is not only improper, but also unacceptable given our current understanding of the powerful potential of neural plasticity and intellectual reserve!

Specifics of a Proactive Lifestyle for Brain Health

This chapter now turns to more specific tips for personal change and for incorporating our own proactive approach towards brain health. Each of us must look at our behavior and evaluate the health promotion value of our current lifestyle. With constructive introspection and analysis of our current lifestyle, we will be able to make specific positive changes where necessary.

The time to begin creating change in personal lifestyle and adopting a proactive lifelong lifestyle that promotes brain health is now! One major myth is that neurodegenerative disorders begin in late life and therefore we do not need to be concerned yet. A second major myth is that diseases are all genetic and our behavior and environment have no bearing on our health. We must understand that we have a tremendous responsibility and opportunity regarding our individual health. It is critical that we understand our role in our own health promotion as primary and that dedication to a healthy lifestyle must begin today.

Ten behaviors are proposed as primary if not critical components to a lifelong lifestyle for brain health (see below and inside back cover). These behaviors are pulled from existing research on aging from the biological, psychological, social, and gerontological sciences. It is important to recall that our brain does not operate in isolation from the rest of the body. Rather, as pointed out in this book the human body operates as a symphony producing a behavioral harmony of life. The heart has a particularly important relationship with the brain with nearly 25% of the oxygen and blood from every heartbeat designated for the brain. Accordingly, some of the lifestyle behaviors proposed for brain health have similar benefit for the cardiovascular system.

Lifestyle Behavior 1: Do not Smoke

Smoking is bad for our health, increases the risk for

cancer, and can lead to an early death. Cancer itself is the second leading cause of death after heart disease and smoking represents a risk factor for both heart disease and stroke. Of concern is the fact that many children begin smoking at an early age often because of peer pressure. Cigarette smoking is a highly controlling behavior and despite whether it should be considered an addiction or not there is significant difficulty stopping smoking once begun. Physicians will plead with their patients to stop smoking or death will likely occur. Despite this serious warning the patient cannot stop the behavior. This represents an extremely unfortunate and yet unique reality. There may not be any other legal behavior where a patient cannot stop a damaging behavior even though they understand that such behavior will likely cause their death. This indicates how hard it must be to stop smoking cigarettes and it further necessitates our need to be supportive of those who are trying to stop. Finally, as parents we must remain vigilant and assertive regarding our children's behavior. There should be no compromise regarding smoking behavior by our children as this behavior once started may not stop and surely will enhance the risk of cancer and premature death.

Lifestyle Behavior 2:
Maintain regular physical examinations and follow your physician's advice

We need to take control of our health and this begins by understanding that we are in charge of the management of our bodies. I am struck by how often this relatively obvious point is not supported by some. There are those who believe their physician or some other person is actually responsible for their health and they will defer important decisions to these other parties. We will be well served to remember that physicians and all clinicians are our employees and with regard to our bodies we are the boss!

Once we establish our own role in the management of our health, the importance of a close and trusting relationship with our physician becomes critical. A team approach can help establish a united front against illness and more importantly promote our health. Open communication can help the physician make sound decisions regarding our health and our compliance with the medical regimen is vital. If we have questions pertaining to vitamins, herbs, exercise, hormones, and other potential treatment adjuncts we should address these with our physician. At no time should we take any adjunctive treatments without the knowledge of our physicians, as there may be contraindications that can pose health problems.

Lifestyle Behavior 3:
Learn new information and engage in the complex and novel

Earlier in the book the importance of complex and novel stimuli upon synaptic density and development of a healthy brain potentially resistant to neurodegenerative disease late in life was reviewed. Many individuals attempt to engage in tasks they believe are mentally stimulating. I wish I had a dime every time someone asked me "if I do the crossword puzzle is that good for my brain?" We still do not have an exact formulary for activities that promote brain health. However, in the near future we will be able to specify which activities are valuable for brain health and promotion of synaptic density. We may be able to attach neuropsychological values to each activity based on how much memory, planning, visuospatial skill, language, etc. is involved. For each activity there may be a related value that predicts how much synaptic density is expected for the particular person, what type of neurochemical alteration will occur, and whether neurogenesis is enhanced by engaging in the activity.

Because each person presents with a different background and life experience activities will likely have an idiosyncratic value while others will have a generalized health promoting value. For example, dance and music may have a more significant value for brain health in a person with no such experience compared to one who is an artist. In the same way, reading and writing are activities that promote language sophistication and may represent value that is more general across the human population. Activities that have the highest value for brain health will be those that are novel and complex for the particular person. It is the novel and complex that will challenge the brain, stimulate learning, and promote synaptic density. The reason an activity is complex and novel for someone is precisely because the individual has not practiced the activity, and there is minimal synaptic density for the activity. With practice of the activity, synaptic density increases and what was once novel and complex slowly becomes passive and rote. As this transition from the complex and novel to the rote and passive occurs, the individual must begin to engage in a new activity characterized as novel and complex. This is my definition of lifelong learning!

I advocate the following exercise to those interested in understanding what might be personally novel and complex versus rote and passive: take out a sheet of white paper and divide the paper in half. On the left side of the page place the three or four activities that you enjoy most, are comfortable doing, have fun with, and do most frequently. There is a reason why we repeat activities we enjoy and similarly why we are better at these activities than others. The list generated on the left side of the page represents activities that are rote and passive and do not likely contribute much to our synaptic density. The reason these activities are rote and passive is that we have engaged in them so often that the neural tracts underlying such activity are already well established. There is minimal if any new neuronal development occurring with these overly repeated activities.

Turning to the right side of the page one can list the three or four activities that he or she does not enjoy, does not engage in frequently, are complicated, and are not easy. In fact the person may be inept at these activities. It is precisely these three or four activities on the right side of the page that represent the complex and novel for the person. The reason these activities are not enjoyed and are hard to perform is that there is minimal if any neuronal tracts developed for them. In a literal sense these activities represent a window into the person's brain where neurophysiological retardation exists. New learning and mental stimulation that results in synaptic development can be accomplished by engaging in the activities listed on the right side of the page!

Lifestyle Behavior 4:
Engage in regular exercise to include daily walking

Exercise has emerged as a significant contributor to overall health and a direct lifestyle behavior that helps to counter risk of disease (Cooper, 1994, Rowe & Kahn, 1998). Physical activity defined by exercise has been shown to increase synaptic density in rodents (Van Pragg et al., 1999). Increased synaptic density is a primary factor in intellectual reserve that may help to prevent or delay the onset of neurodegenerative disease in humans. Exercise has been demonstrated to have a positive effect on humans across the lifespan and to enhance successful aging in general (Rowe & Kahn, 1998). Recent studies (Arkin, 2001; Cotman et al., 2002) have also demonstrated the positive effect of exercise upon disease states of the central nervous system: exercise performed on a routine basis may not only reduce the risk of neurodegenerative disease, but may also help to slow the course of an existing disease such as AD.

Despite this, relatively smart people will inform me that they do not have the time to exercise. To combat this common excuse for not exercising, I often suggest parking one's car far from the front door to promote walking greater distances. Instead of using escalators or elevators one should use steps as often as possible. Within our residential and occupational settings we are afforded the opportunity on a daily basis to walk rapidly. Part of this walking will naturally involve climbing steps. With these three small but practical examples, we can exercise on a daily basis as part of our natural daily activity and thereby not require any additional time to exercise.

Building a modest exercise program that features walking can be life extending if not life saving. A brief but brisk walk around the block two to three times a week is a great way to start. Such exercise will afford us more energy, increased psychological well-being, increased feelings of euphoria, better sleep, and enhanced cognition. Given these positive consequences of a modest exercise program one wonders why we refrain from getting started. Introspection enables some insight why we do not exercise and why we may stop once our program has begun. Identifying our personal roadblocks to exercise represents the first step in our removing such personal resistance to a more healthy and robust body and brain. Combating our roadblocks to exercise is not easy. Identification of why we do not exercise, however, permits us to systematically breakdown our resistance and to slowly change our behaviors towards health promotion.

Lifestyle Behavior 5: Socialize, have fun, and slow down

Americans tend to be too hurried, fatigued, and stressed. We continue to develop a society that is faster and faster with greater pressure to keep up for a variety of questionable reasons. There is a real lack of understanding and knowledge regarding the importance of slowing down and relaxing periodically. We underestimate the importance of relaxation, belittle relaxation techniques, and consider vacation time a luxury. Of interest is the fact that most Americans have only one or two weeks out of fifty-two designated to vacation or relax!

As society becomes more technological and hurried the stress level is likely to increase. This book has reviewed research demonstrating the negative effects of chronic stress upon the human body and brain. There may be a relationship between the speed of life and the increased prevalence of attention deficit disorder and hyperactivity relative to fifty years ago. More Americans seek immediate fixes to their ills such as anxiety and depression that are likely secondary to maladaptive coping styles for a stressful life. Utilization of psychotropics has never been greater including use by children. Research has shown that animal brains exposed to environments too enriched and too driven actually resist development (Diamond & Hopson, 1998). The effect of our increasingly fast society upon the health of our brains is not yet understood but the concern should be real.

Reduction of stress from our lives is not complicated though it certainly involves change. Once again, lifestyle is the critical agent in need of change. As Americans we do not like change. Consider the idea of sitting at a different chair around the dinner table tonight or sleeping on a different side of the bed. These are not life-threatening challenges and yet they represent difficult changes for a significant number of us. Projecting this type of change to the effort required for starting an exercise program, eating healthier, and spending more time in enjoyable activities might be staggering! Despite our resistance to change and our obsessed inclination to be stressed we must confront and accept the idea that reduction of stress from our lives involves slowing down and using our time more intelligently!

I encourage people to make a list of the three to five things that are most stressful to them in their lives. Typically, the list includes something to do with occupation and something to do with having too much responsibility. My anecdotal experience with this exercise is that people generally are not conscious of their daily choices and instead are painfully aware of the consequences of their choices. Consequences such as fatigue, poor sleep and dietary routines, little exercise, interpersonal problems, excessive use of nicotine, alcohol, and illegal drugs, mood disorders, anxiety, and neglect of loved ones are too common. A primary reason we have too much to do in life is that we have not taken the time to prioritize what is most important to us. As such, I always ask persons to make a list of the three to five things (or people) that are most important to them, those things that they would like to spend more time doing. With this information we can begin to assess not only what triggers our stress but also what keeps us from engaging in activities and pursuits that are more enjoyable, less stressful.

A common theme regarding our decisions in life that result in stress is our lack of assertiveness. Because we do not consciously know, or we behave in ways to suggest we do not know, what environmental factors contribute to our stress we develop patterns of behavior that lead to maladaptive routine and repetition. Decisions that follow a routine and lead to stress are not health promoting. Our listing of stressors is one small step to make the process conscious, to better identify and understand environmental factors that are stressful to us and unhealthy. Our conscious identification of potential stressors can lead to better decision making to stay away and minimize our exposure to these stressors. Ultimately, however, our ability to limit our exposure to stressful environments depends on our ability to say "no." There is real power in our ability to say no to another responsibility, to participate in activities that we know will result in our becoming overwhelmed and overloaded.

Reducing demands we place on ourselves is a critical step towards stress reduction. We may be surprised that a significant amount of what we do is not necessary in the larger scheme of life. We may fall prey to exaggeration of the importance of what we do or to the importance of our role in some activity. A critical priority that is neglected throughout our daily decision making process is our health. While our brains permit us to process complex, multiple types of information rapidly, our brains also require some time to process information more deeply and to introspect. This can be accomplished by being alone and thinking, by engaging in recreation, and by increasing the number of hours we sleep in a day! Our brains consolidate information during sleep and yet many Americans report fatigue and sleep disorders. Implementing naps as part of our daily routines (even 20 minute sleep periods) and corporate culture would probably result in a more energetic and positive work force.

Learning how to relax is a curiously difficulty technique for Americans. We actually have developed a big business around ways to relax. Simply put, we need to carve out "our time" during the day when we will do nothing more than become in tune with ourselves. Certainly, breathing is a critical component to relaxation as slowing the breathing down to become more rhythmical typically leads to slowed physiology. In turn, we feel better and our psychology becomes healthier. Meditation, prayer, yoga, and more formal relaxation procedures are methods to guide us towards relaxed states (Koenig, 1995; Rowe & Kahn, 1998; Snowdon, 2001). I recommend such techniques for fifteen to twenty minutes three times a day. This will help to slow our hectic schedule and hurried pace that result in a cumulative negative effect on the body (Cooper, 1994).

We can also reduce stress in our lives by dedicating parts of the day and the week to ourselves. Those things that are fun for us should be prioritized over the things that are stress producing. This may involve some minor shifting of time and delegation or it may demand a significant decision to leave a given occupation. Surveys typically indicate many Americans are not happy with their current jobs. Despite the type of change necessary, dedication to self and to others important in our lives is critical. Consider how much time is allotted to play, to leisure, and to activities that will foster laughter and joy. Compare that to how much time we allot to activities that foster tension, irritability, and internalization of stress. The current balance of joy to stress is not favorable to our health. We need to change and to make conscious decisions to allocate more time to those experiences that are fun and to allocate more available time for ourselves in general. One simple message to take seriously is to *slow down*!

Lifestyle Behavior 6:
Be financially stable and hire a financial planner

We know that having some money left in late life correlates with health (Torres-Gil, 1992). This does not infer the need to save millions of dollars but rather conveys the importance of saving enough money to live comfortably. Research also indicates that while there is no greater amount of poverty in late life relative to young adults, women at both young and older ages are at increased risk for poverty relative to men. This reality becomes underscored because women outlive men on average by nearly six years in the United States. The issue of financial planning becomes a health promotions issue because a well developed plan for financial security in late life promotes health. I often encourage those in my workshops to call a financial planner to begin this process. Financial planners, like teachers, do not consider themselves as health care providers but they really are. It is not a bad idea to take someone younger than you with you to the financial planner. This will give the younger person a chance perhaps you did not have and initiate their health promotions plan earlier in life.

Lifestyle Behavior 7:
Be spiritual and engage in daily prayer or meditation

The importance of formalized prayer and religiosity on our health is becoming more apparent and understood (Koenig, 1995; Snowdon, 2001). Studies have documented a relationship between prayer and immune system, to longevity and attendance at formalized places of worship, and to the general well being of those who may be ill. Despite these and other findings on the potential power of prayer to health, we have not integrated such behavior into the mainstream of our "health care system." For example, we typically do not have a section of the medical chart dedicated to religious or spiritual discipline. Also, it is rare to have a religious leader as part of the interdisciplinary team of health care professionals charged with the development of care plans for patients. It is unheard of for a physician to write a prescription for the "Our Father."

As more Americans demand more options from the traditional highly medicalized health care system of today, one should not be too surprised to find meditation or prayer find its way into some of our health insurance programs. A whole new field of study referred to as "neurotheology" has been advanced to study the neurophysiological correlates of prayer and meditation. As our understanding of this relationship emerges our ability to apply such knowledge in a health-promoting manner may become available. The day of Mediprayer is not far away!

Lifestyle Behavior 8: Eat less and include antioxidants

The importance of what we eat on our health, behavior, and mood cannot be overstated (Cooper, 1994; Kotulak, 1997; Null, 2000; Rowe & Kahn, 1998). The extent of information in this area is beyond the scope of this book and only briefly reviewed here. The foods that we choose to eat enter our body, have some impact, and then leave our body. Clearly, there is going to be consequences to our health based on the types of foods we choose to enter our body. We are all familiar with the need for diets that include the recommended daily consumption of the four food groups. One major problem we have as Americans is our over-consumption of food. Animal research has established a strong relationship between generalized caloric restriction and longevity (Lee, C. K., Klopp, R. G., Weindruch, R., & Prolla, T. A., 1999; Null, 2000).

Two of my physicians provided me advice earlier in my life when I did not understand the idea of caloric restriction. The first advice was to not go to bed feeling stuffed from eating. The second advice was to consume only 80% of what I intend to eat at every meal. Such advice is practical, wise, and useful as a general guide. Perhaps the advice given me by my doctors will be useful to you. The reasons we eat are numerous and many do not relate to nutrition. Understanding why we eat and what we eat is a critical component to our health.

Caloric restriction and longevity is not considered conclusive in humans as in animals. However, given our tendency to over-consume the results from the animal research are concerning. Generalized caloric reduction under the supervision of our physicians is probably a good idea. The physician will help to make sure we maintain the necessary daily nutritional intake while reducing the maladaptive behavior of overeating.

As part of our fast paced culture we have created food businesses known as fast-food restaurants. We literally have reinforced speed of food consumption and eating on the run both of which are not health promoting. The types of foods that we eat can be detrimental to our health particularly when we consume foods high in processed fats and fried foods. A lifestyle of passivity with unhealthy diets is precisely a major reason why our children are obese at unprecedented rates. Studies indicate children spend more time in front of the television than they do at school or with their parents (Diamond & Hopson, 1998).

Foods that may be brain health promoting include omega-3 fatty acids such as salmon and almonds. Similarly, foods with naturally occurring vitamin E and Vitamin C have been found to be healthy secondary to their antioxidant effect (Cooper, 1994). Folate has been found to be a powerfully healthy vitamin as it occurs naturally in some foods and may even help to reduce the risk of some neurodegenerative illnesses and developmental disorders (Cooper, 1994; Null, 2000). A glass of red wine with a meal has been found to not only help as an anti-atherosclerotic beverage but to potentially help with cognition (Corder et al. 2001; Orgogozo, 1997). This is not hard to understand given our knowledge of the close relationship between cardiac health and brain health. Red wine has also been found to have potentially more health promoting benefit than other types of alcohol (Gronbaek, et al. 2000). Grape juice as a substitute for wine has been discussed as potentially helpful with regard to health.

The field of nutrition and brain health has not advanced to the point of specifying the "Brain Diet." However, we know that some reduction in food intake while maintaining proper daily nutrition, foods with antioxidants, and foods that help our cardiovascular system and blood flow are most likely beneficial to our central nervous systems.

Another way to think about the health promoting effects of diet is to consider the psychosocial importance of the meal itself. Most of us will celebrate an important day or event in our life by eating dinner at our favorite restaurant. Typically the restaurant has a nice ambience with the expected lighting, music, good service, and nice décor that goes to the enjoyment of the dinner. Company of other humans is quite customary and likely necessary to make the meal most satisfying; remember socialization is important. We can all relate to the positive effects of such an activity. Now compare that with the typical meal in our nursing homes across the country where the primary measure of outcome is whether or not the food arrives on the unit warm. There is minimal if any consideration for ambience, service is not framed from a hospitality objective, and the timing of meals is typically based more on staff schedule than resident or patient desire. We are significantly poor in our understanding and use of the meal as a health promoting intervention in the long-term care industry of America.

Towards this end I wonder what it would take for our nation to guarantee that every nursing home maintains a chef as standard to the care of our older Americans. This is particularly critical when one considers that the entire day for a resident of any nursing home is based on the meal. Food is paramount to older adults in nursing homes and my observation has been that food is more important to most persons as we age, regardless of health. To date, however, we have not formally considered diet and the important psychosocial factors of food and the meal within the context of health promotion.

Lifestyle Behavior 9:
Maintain strong family and friendship networks

Interestingly, most of us will list family and love to be important if not critical components to our quality of life and health. Clearly, damage is done to our health and illness ensues after death of a loved one or after a family divorce. These real world examples support the importance of family and love in our lives. Despite their importance to our health they are rarely considered when money is provided for "preventative programs."

Humans require love and need to express love. Typically love is expressed to other humans though for some love may be expressed to pets or even a stuffed animal. Residents of nursing homes who have dementia exemplify the latter. The target of their affection may be a stuffed animal though the intensity of their love is tremendous. Even when the brain is invaded by neurodegenerative disorders there remains a need to love that we presently do not understand and certainly do not consider health promoting.

Part of staying involved in society and maintaining a complex and novel environment for our brains to thrive is sustaining a network of friends. Research demonstrates the importance of a social network in reducing the risk of dementia (Fratiglioni, Wang, Ericsson, Maytan, & Winblad, 2000). As we get older friends may take the place of family members who have died. Our ability to communicate with and interact with a network of friends is critical. Friends provide opportunities and enable a sharing of experiences. From friendship come learning, challenge, emotion, trust, and understanding. Role development often occurs when friends engage in new pursuits and friendship can provide the necessary motivation towards activity and involvement.

Development of strong family and friendships is not a given nor is it easy. However, as part of the lifestyle for a healthy brain the importance of proactive nurturing of relationships cannot be underestimated. We can maintain close communication with our family members thereby fueling a loving bond. With more communication tools at our disposal than ever there is little reason not to make weekly contact with our parents and siblings. Family activities are another method to advance the powerful health promoting force of love and an annual family reunion is a good idea.

Community is a general term that conveys a gathering of people. Our society provides many vehicles for such community. Places of worship, parent-teacher organizations, sports, clubs, and entertainment represent some of the forums where we can participate and develop relations with other people. Such activities also provide us with an opportunity to enjoy, laugh, and have fun. These types of activities are health promoting as they offer stress reduction, new learning, and emotional expression. Though we do not completely understand the health promoting effect of family, friendship, or community they clearly are important to humans and most likely contribute to our well being in ways we do not appreciate. We are not meant to be alone and isolation is bad for our health. Our ability to continually develop relations and sustain them across the lifespan represents a real proactive, health promoting behavior.

Lifestyle Behavior 10:
Do not retire from life and maintain a role and purpose

Human beings and the brains of human beings should never retire. Despite foolish legislation that financially incentivizes Americans to withdraw and isolate, this book champions a lifelong pursuit of new learning, socialization, and engagement. Retirement cannot foster novel and complex environments the way continued involvement in society does. A conscious decision to stay actively involved is a good idea that further conveys a proactive approach to lifelong brain health. Part of this decision making process is the development of a forward looking, positive attitude. Attitude most likely plays a significant role not only in general success in life but in health and ability to recover from illness (Lewis, Dennis, O'Rourke, & Sharpe, 2001).

In order to maintain involvement and strong participation in society across the lifespan it is important to develop multiple skills and interests early in life. Development of hobbies and talents can be tremendously helpful particularly when society reinforces removal from the workforce. Having a reason for getting up each day should never be underestimated and a role and purpose in life are critical components to longevity. It is our responsibility to nurture different roles and developing ourselves as persons with many purposes.

Older Americans are turning to the higher education system in retirement. School is an excellent example of one purpose and for many older people their day is filled with academic curiosity. The university milieu can be a powerful health promoting environment for the brain including the older brain. More older adults are developing new talents (Cohen, 2001) such as music and painting to the point where studies are underway to better understand the apparent relationship between creativity and advanced age. That talents emerge late in life supports neural plasticity and contradicts the traditional belief that the brain has little capacity late in life.

More older persons are returning to work at least on a part-time basis than ever before. The role of work in our culture is significant not only for the economics but for psychological reasons. We identify strongly with our jobs even though many of us are not happy with them. Work may be a necessary activity for human beings and provide more meaning to our overall condition than we appreciate. Clearly, the loss of a job can cause significant effects to our economic and psychological health suggesting the presence of work is health promoting. Matching our passions in life with an occupation is powerful and can promote our talents and potential in significant ways. Despite this many are not confident enough to pursue their passions and instead remain trapped in a work environment where they are not happy.

As we get older and our social network expands we may develop new roles and a new purpose. This can be healthy particularly since the novel typically is complex and both are critical to human brain health. The major points of this lifestyle behavior are that we need to stay involved to grow and to develop, that retirement is not a healthy choice unless there are sufficient hobbies and talents to maintain a role, and that pursuit of our passions will likely provide the greatest return in personal development.

Lifestyle by definition demands vigilance and change. Indeed, successful aging, as defined by the oldest old, is the process of adaptation not a physical state (Von Faber et al. 2001.) As Americans we do not like to change particularly when it involves difficulty and burden. Lifestyle change is relatively difficult when approached from this perspective and most of us will fail once or twice in the process. Nonetheless, the proactive lifestyle advocated by this book is lifelong and therefore continuous. Our attempts to develop a healthier lifestyle will be ongoing and different lifestyle behaviors may demand more time and effort than others. The importance of initiating change is that we become an active participant in our own health.

While no clearly documented scientific formulary yet exists for brain health the lifestyle proposed by this book is no less important. It is critical that the concept of lifestyle for brain health be reinforced and adopted as part of our national health policy. Our developing understanding of the human brain as a dynamic and reorganizing system makes a proactive lifestyle necessary for brain health. In addition, our understanding that brain degeneration caused by conditions such as Alzheimer's disease begin to erode the brain early in life turns such a lifestyle into a potential defense system. Most importantly, this book champions such a proactive lifestyle for brain health because it empowers each individual with the opportunity to change and to adopt new more healthy behaviors believed to have a positive influence on development of synaptic density and intellectual reserve.

Conclusion

The human brain is the most magnificent system in the universe. Our understanding of the complexity and efficiency of the brain is really still at a primitive level. We have attempted to explain brain function using models of the telephone lines and computers. These have not worked simply because there is no model that parallels the sophistication of the human brain. Research into the fundamental structure and function of the brain is ongoing at a furious pace. The nineties was declared "decade of the brain" by the United States and we have learned much. However, there remains significant tension and disagreement regarding the true ability of the human brain.

Neural plasticity is a relatively new concept as it applies to the human brain. This book used neural plasticity to refer to a brain that is highly dynamic, constantly reorganizing, and malleable. Plasticity enables a system to change, develop, and to regenerate. Such ideas run counter to the established principle that the human brain is fixed, rigid and essentially on a deteriorating course from birth. The two competing ideas of brain capacity, plasticity versus rigidity, lie at the heart of the current academic tension.

There is little debate regarding the presence of plasticity in the brains of rodents and nonhuman primates into adulthood. The hippocampus and olfactory system have been found to be areas of the animal's brain capable of neurogenesis. Debate remains regarding whether higher order cortical areas also have capacity for neurogenesis and this answer will be forthcoming. Plasticity in the form of neurogenesis in the hippocampus of the animal's brain is significant. The hippocampus is a critical brain structure that enables encoding of new information thereby initiating the formation of new memories. Learning itself is one outcome of such brain function. Given that the hippocampus represents the encoder of all new information into the brain, it is relatively easy to appreciate not only its importance but also its need to have plasticity; from a Darwinian perspective the hippocampus would need to regenerate. The fact that animals have demonstrated neurogenesis in any area of the brain raises fundamental questions not the least of which is why does the human brain not have this same capacity? Indeed, why does a rat brain have some capacity our brain does not?

This fundamental question drove the writing of this book. It is my belief that regardless of where our current science is on the matter it makes no logical sense for the human brain not to have the same properties of plasticity as the rat brain! Our inability to measure the presence of such plasticity is a separate matter from the argument of its existence and should not be confused. This book has highlighted research on the human brain that demonstrates new ways of understanding our central nervous system primarily because of our increased ability to measure the function and structure of the brain. As our technology for measuring the human brain advances we will likely witness a completely new understanding and approach to the brain, one that includes plasticity and neurogenesis as major principles.

This book reviewed research on plasticity and neurogenesis in the animal brain. The significance of an enriched environment was supported and the important components to such an environment were reviewed. These included socialization, physical exercise, and mental stimulation. The research reviewed was clear and consistent on this point: animals raised in an enriched environment have significantly more brain cells and synaptic activity in their hippocampi than animals raised in a standard and more sterile environment. The animal research demonstrates a clear and direct relationship between environmental enrichment and brain morphology. As noted above, the extent of this relationship is now under review and may include brain regions beyond the hippocampus.

Given the direct relationship between environment and morphology of the animal brain, the necessary question becomes "does the same relationship exist for the human brain"? This book reviewed two studies that report neurogenesis in the human brain. Of significance is the finding of neurogenesis in the hippocampi of the human brain, the same region of neurogenesis found in the animal brain. While two studies are not enough to draw firm conclusions on the issue of neurogenesis in the human brain there is clear momentum in the field for such a finding. Neurogenesis in the human brain and empirical support for the impact of environment on the morphology and function of the human brain represent two critically significant issues for the human condition and human race.

This book underscores the importance of the animal brain research and highlights the early findings on neurogenesis in the human brain to propose the concept of brain health. Framed conceptually from a health perspective, neurogenesis and neuronal plasticity offers us a new opportunity to understand the human brain from a developmental and health promoting approach. Similar to our understanding and approach to health promotion of the cardiovascular system we are now poised to apply environments and personal behaviors that promote the health and well being of our central nervous system. From this conceptualization a lifestyle for the health of the human brain was proposed and defined by this book.

This book does not presume that the specific lifestyle for brain health exists. However, turning to the research on the animal brain we can apply important findings to develop such a lifestyle. Environment appears to be important regarding the development and shape of our brains. Environmental factors such as socialization, physical activity, and mental stimulation were found to be important for neurogenesis in the animal brain. These same factors are proposed as important to the human brain and to maximizing the potential for human brain development, neurogenesis and synaptic activity in the human brain, and ultimately brain health. The theory supporting such ideas is known as intellectual reserve and suggests that the enrichment of the environment affects brain morphology by increasing synaptic density, itself a potential measure of brain integrity. Intellectual reserve has been proposed as a potential defense against neurodegenerative disorders either by preventing or delaying its onset. Regardless, the idea that environment affects intellectual reserve and that intellectual reserve may fight off brain disease is one clear example of how neural plasticity may be applied towards health promotion.

For the human brain this book promotes a lifelong lifestyle towards brain health. Research yields environmental factors that relate to reduced risk of neurodegenerative disease and therefore provide reasonable ingredients for consideration of such a lifestyle. Some of the major environmental factors include increased education, parental love and nurturance, enhanced occupation, higher intelligence quotients, self-seeking of stimulation at an early age, language development early in life, ongoing learning, physical exercise, reduction of stress and passivity, socialization, healthy diet, and minimization of the risk factors associated with heart disease.

These environmental factors are not new and some have already been discussed with regard to our general health. However, placing these factors within a lifestyle that promotes the health of the human brain is new. This book proposes methods to integrate these environmental factors into programs and institutions that already exist. One example articulated in the supplemental policy chapter (next chapter) of this book is to reconceptualize our educational system towards a wellness center for the human brain where curriculum is developed to grow specific brain regions, to enhance IQ, and to increase synaptic density. Another example (see supplemental policy chapter) is for our health insurance companies to include lifelong learning as part of every preventative health package. Payment for such learning pursuits reinforces the idea that such mental stimulation is health promoting and while it may not prevent disease it may help to slow the onset and course of neurodegeneration. Our children and infants may benefit from exposure to environments that stimulate language development through sign language prior to oral language, training and reinforcement of children's self initiated mental stimulation, and enhancement of IQ at early ages. These factors can be part of every Head Start program supported and reinforced by our nation. Finally, our government may reconsider our current understanding and approach to "retirement" since it appears to be detrimental to brain health. Passivity and isolation are not good for the health of the brain. A national policy that reinforces such behavior deserves scrutiny and alteration to align itself with our new understanding of brain health.

Throughout the research undertaken for this book there emerged some basic principles regarding human brain health. First, brain health promotion is a lifelong process. Our early environments appear to be critical and may represent a type of *neuronal catapult* across our lifespan. Early environments rich in those factors proposed for brain health may enable significant brain development with extensive synaptic activity to defend against potential neuronal insult. This book proposed the idea that conditions such as Alzheimer's disease that manifest clinically in late life may actually begin to invade the brain in childhood if not earlier. Building a robust brain therefore would seem to be an important strategy at the earliest of ages. Second, the human brain responds well to novelty and complexity. Novelty and complexity may underlie the health value for every activity we engage in and brain health may be maximized if we engage in activities that are both novel and complex to us. In contrast, environments that foster passive and rote activities will not be healthy to our brains. At the core of mental stimulation are activities rich in novelty and complexity. Interestingly, as pointed out in this book, those activities that are initially novel and complex eventually become rote and passive as our brains develop neuronal pathways—synaptic density—with practice.

This is a perfect time in our evolution to forward the importance of brain health, to champion a national policy that supports the health and development of our brains, and to apply direct policies and behaviors that promote brain health. This book represents another small step in this important direction. Enriched environments beginning early in life and maintained across the lifespan are critical to overall brain health. Such a conceptual shift requires policy change and personal change to reinforce lifestyle as important to brain health. Personal responsibility is critical in the same way that personal behavior is important to cardiovascular health. Today, the public does not necessarily consider brain health in the same way we consider cardiovascular health. This book joins other forces to make brain health salient and a priority. Our demographic shift indicates an aging population vulnerable to multiple conditions including brain disease. A proactive approach that reinforces a health promoting lifestyle for the human brain is essential and needed at this time.

In writing this book it became clear that research on the human brain represents an exploding area of inquiry and understanding. As this conclusion is drafted ideas are expressed at scientific meetings and in publications across the world that support the concept of a lifestyle for the human brain: mental exercise in the form of cognitively stimulating activities may be associated with reduced risk of Alzheimer's (Verghese et al., 2003; Wilson et al., 2002); an active and challenging life leads to neurogenesis in the hippocampi of older mice (Kempermann, 2002); and exercise in humans may activate plasticity at the synaptic and cellular level thereby protecting against age-related insults (Cotman & Berchtold, 2002). Perhaps the greatest support for this book's concept of a lifelong, health-promoting lifestyle for the human brain is the discussion of such at the meeting of the International Alzheimer's Association in Sweden in 2002.

Overall, the realm of brain health is new and filled with opportunity and promise. With advances in our neuroimaging technologies we will discover the true miracle that is the human brain. It will be interesting to witness whether we become so enthralled with the technology that simply demonstrates the complexity of the brain to not recognize that the method to affect brain morphology and function (brain health) may actually be simplistic and easy! I am reminded of the messages provided me by my parents many years ago: "If you have nothing good to say don't open your mouth," "get busy," "think for yourself," "study hard and good things will happen," and "don't take any shortcuts." These messages may have more meaning than I ever considered. From the perspective of brain health the messages reinforce the importance of novelty and complexity and infer the power of environmental input (good and bad) upon the integrity of the brain. At the heart of science is parsimony and perhaps in the end we will not only discover the power of the human brain but that the means to unleash this power may rely upon the simple and basic lifestyle proposed in this book.

Starting today be proactive and begin to expose your brain to the most complex and novel environment possible. Initiate your proactive lifestyle and make the necessary changes to promote your brain health. Such healthy choices likely will lead to increased synaptic density that will help to minimize your risk of neurodegeneration and thereby guarantee that you **never lose your wonderful life story**!

A Policy Perspective on Health and Aging

Supplemental

Some ideas are now presented to foster a culture that prioritizes the importance of being proactive and of maintaining a lifelong lifestyle for brain health. Such a culture involves general and conceptual changes that will require time and patience. Interestingly, the type of policy initiatives proposed do not require the invention of anything new but rather a re-conceptualization of what already exists. The major underlying principle guiding the conceptual shift is proactive health promotion rather than our current approach of reactivity and disease.

I.   Mental Stimulation

Enriched environments demonstrate a direct positive morphological effect on the animal brain, both in synaptic density and cortical mass (Diamond & Hopson, 1998). This

149

effect is documented to occur from an early period in the animal's life into adulthood. For humans, the critical issue is how to create enriched environments at the earliest age of development to trigger a healthy developing central nervous system that will compound health value across the lifespan. While most of the research has documented the detrimental effects of head injury, stress, poverty, nutritional deficiency, lack of parental involvement and drug abuse on the developing brain, little research has focused on the positive effects of a positive environment. Diamond and Hopson (1998) provided an overview of the importance of early mental stimulation for the healthy development of babies and toddlers in addition to the need for care and nurturing. Such an environment has particular importance at the earliest of age because the brain is developing so rapidly at infancy and will be molded to a significant degree based on environmental input. This book reviewed work by Moceri et al., (2000) that demonstrated the potential for brain devastation when a child's environment is not enriched. Given the premise that early environments are critical to the developing central nervous system in humans it makes practical sense to consider initiatives that promote enriched environments at the earliest of ages.

The Enriched Womb

Environmental enrichment should occur at the earliest stage of human development within the womb (Nathanielsz, 1999). Indeed the environment of the womb may represent the launch pad for a lifelong lifestyle towards brain health. The wonderful human brain weighing somewhere between two and four pounds at maturity and utilizing nearly 25% of the body's energy develops long before the baby emerges from mother's womb. The billions of brain cells that form the higher order part of the human brain known as the cortex begin the developmental process as early as one week after an egg has been fertilized. There is a highly competitive storm of events across the nine-month developmental process that results in a central nervous system ripe for growth. Throughout the developmental period in the womb, however, stimulating environments may be important beyond what is known today.

Research on the impact of nurturing environmental input to the developing fetus and embryo is inconclusive. There is little doubt that substance abuse, physical trauma, and emotional distress can damage a developing fetus. Despite the fact that we do not yet completely understand the value of a nurturing environment upon the fetus in the womb, it is reasonable to underscore research that stress on the developing fetus will cause retardation of many of the major organ systems in the body including the brain. Proper diet by the mother is critical during pregnancy for similar reasons. In general, the developing brain appears to thrive with development of neurons, glial cells, and cellular connectivity when exposed to an active but non threatening environment (Nathanielsz, 1999). The critical question remains how do we identify and then foster the proper environment for brain development in the womb?

As our medical technology advances we will produce the

capacity to measure environmental input on the development of the fetus and embryo developing in the womb. This will spawn an entirely new field of research and clinical practice designed to foster healthy newborns and robust brains from an enriched womb. Early prenatal education can include curriculum that teaches the parents the importance of environment and environmental input on the womb and their developing fetus. Similarly, parents of a developing fetus will benefit from knowledge of what the enriched womb is and why an enriched environment is important across the lifespan.

The Early Child Years and Language for Brain Health

This book reviewed literature that described the importance of language development, learning through education, and intelligence for the developing brain. These three factors and others are significantly important to the child's brain for it is in these highly sensitive years of brain development that a potentially healthy lifestyle can be reinforced. While studies have reported the importance of nurturing environments upon brain and body development including an association between duration of breastfeeding and adult intelligence (Mortensen et al., 2002) early *cognitive catapults* for brain health have not been as readily discussed.

One major cognitive function with potential for brain health promotion across the lifespan is language development. Clearly, the human brain begins to manifest a need to communicate orally from about one year of age. Gestural symbols may be displayed first, but as the child continues to grow and is exposed to more verbalization, the brain rapidly develops the capacity and need to speak orally. Language development is not only a practical necessity it is a fundamental health promoting behavior.

Language and the development of language have typically not been considered health issues. As the major information processing system in the universe, however, the human brain relies heavily if not primarily on the use of language. This suggests that language itself might represent a far more significant process than simply a form of natural cognitive development. The brain's need for language and the brain's reaction to language development may be considered as health promoting as any aerobic workout for the heart. Given this presumption, language development that leads to increased language acumen may indeed represent one early marker of a well-developed brain (see Snowdon et al., 1996).

That language development might represent a health promoting behavior indicates a need to intervene early in life to begin nurturing the language system. For most humans, the left dominant hemisphere is primarily responsible for language. Interestingly, deaf persons who may rely on sign language to communicate utilize nearly the identical language structures in the brain used by hearing persons. This is of particular interest as research indicates that babies, prior to onset of oral language, use gestural symbols or sign language (Acredolo & Goodwyn, 2000). Research has further demonstrated hearing babies can learn multiple signs and that these babies, compared to controls, have higher levels of intelligence several years later (Acredolo & Goodwyn, 2000). This suggests that sign language may be a practical tool that nurtures the language structures in the brain prior to onset of oral language leading to increased intelligence. Given the important relationship of intelligence on brain health promotion and reduced risk of dementia later in life (reviewed earlier), it is proposed therefore that **sign language** be taught to babies prior to onset of oral language. From a policy perspective, sign language or symbolic gestures can be part of every baby wellness or head start program in the United States. Much the same way babies require vaccinations against measles, mumps, and rubella, sign language should be taught prior to onset of oral language.

Separate studies have indicated a significant relationship between intelligence as measured by Intelligence Quotient (IQ) and reduced risk of AD and other dementias in later life (Plassman et al. 1995; Whalley et al. 2000). Other studies have documented a robust correlation between level of education defined by number of years in school and reduced risk of AD and other dementias in later life (Schmand et al., 1997; Stern et al., 1992, 1994, 1995). Further, occupation level, independent of education, has been found to correlate inversely with risk of AD (Jorm et al., 1998). Each of these studies points to the importance of intellectual reserve theory and its potential practical application to brain health. Indeed, increasing synaptic density by increasing the number of years that one is exposed to education and learning, by increasing intelligence and by increasing the sophistication of work conducted in the occupational setting, may be considered proactive initiatives for brain health.

A common factor that is woven through these research findings is language development. Clearly, a more sophisticated language system typically yields higher IQ, advancement in the educational system, and greater opportunity in the employment world. Higher socioeconomic status typically results and overall health is generally better. From a health promotion perspective therefore, language development aggressively and early in life is critically important not only to develop a robust brain, but also to potentially enable the brain to delay manifestation of neurodegeneration many years later.

The Education System as a Wellness Center for the Brain

The rather extensive literature supporting a relationship between increased years of education and lowered risk of neurodegenerative disease warrants attention to our school system and learning system in the country. To date, education has generally not been conceptualized as a health promoting or health demoting entity. This author proposes a re-conceptualization of our educational system as a "wellness center for the human brain." The buildings we call schools and the campuses of learning we refer to as colleges and universities may have significant import to brain health. Settings of our schools, colleges, and universities across the nation represent enriched environments capable of promoting novelty and complexity and thereby facilitating intellectual reserve.

The educational system is intended to provide an

environment rich in mental stimulation. Though not designed for health, the schools and universities of our country are one example of centers for brain health similar to aerobic centers for the heart. The socialization aspect of school is likely important, but the cognitive demands of learning most likely represent the major contributor of education towards brain health. Cognitively, our education system is intended to provide a natural environment rich in novelty and complexity. These factors were discussed earlier as major tenets of intellectual reserve important for maintaining and spawning neuronal health.

Important to any discussion of our educational system and brain health is the curriculum that is developed and taught to the children and young adults across the nation. Curriculum has not been developed with health in mind. Rather, curriculum is developed and implemented to foster advancement of students to the next level of cognitive proficiency. Curriculum development might be conceptualized better from the perspective of brain health and wellness. Imagine developing specific curriculum to promote brain development in specific and general ways. There may be certain curriculum with certain teaching modalities that promotes regional brain development. In contrast, curriculum might be developed to promote more general brain growth. The primary outcome of this approach is to develop healthy brains. Secondary outcomes would include good grades and passing to the next level of brain development. From this context, schools represent a primary setting for direct promotion of brain health.

Teachers alone cannot develop curriculum for brain health. Unfortunately, curriculum within the school systems is developed and controlled by teachers who have little training or background on the human brain. A more enlightened approach to curriculum development for healthy brains is to have teachers work with neuroscientists, speech and language experts, cognitive specialists, neuroimaging experts, research teams, etc. This team approach would enable the development of curriculum that intends to develop the human brain and that can be measured for such outcomes.

To further support this education initiative it is proposed that school settings be equipped with the latest functional neuroimaging technology. This would permit measurement of the effect of curriculum and teaching approach upon the development of the student's brain. Functional neuroimaging is a useful tool for measuring development and change and also for providing outcome data to guide teaching and curriculum. It makes no sense to use our most sophisticated neuroimaging technologies only to detect the presence or absence of disease. Such a medicalized approach offers no promise for proactive brain health promotion. Design of settings with appropriate curriculum and utilization of measurement tools to support established health promoting goals is one way to advance our school systems as primary settings of brain health across the lifespan.

Some critics of this initiative may raise concerns regarding the financing of such an expensive endeavor. Clearly there will be resistance by the teacher's union to share development of curriculum. Some may even question who will manage the neuroimaging machines and interpretation of results? While each of these criticisms has merit it is important to recognize our current situation regarding brain disease in this country. For all of the billions of dollars we spend annually in direct and indirect costs for AD we have but four medications approved by the Federal Drug Administration. We have developed a long-term nursing home industry that is avoided by most Americans, and we have no chronic care system. Shifting existing, redundant expenditures from the medical world to the educational world (and vice versa) appears to worthwhile if only to pilot this idea initially. My sense is that real dollars could be saved by integrating these two large expenditures into one when appropriate. There is no reason why radiologists cannot contract with schools or be paid for by third party insurance carriers as they are now within the medical system. This approach is based on our nation understanding that health services need not be reactive or medicalized and that payment for health promoting behaviors (curriculum development and imaging outcome data in schools) is one example of being proactive. Finally, if our agenda for development of robust brains early in life is pure there should be no threat from external political, personal, union, or other agendas.

A Learning Vaccine across the Lifespan

Closer analysis of this education initiative suggests the need to also re-conceptualize learning itself. Most likely, the buildings and classroom design has little positive effect on intellectual reserve. However, learning that occurs within the variety of settings referred to as schools deserves attention. Learning itself may represent a critical behavior for brain health promotion. Traditional learning is viewed as a means to an end that usually includes a grade, diploma, and perhaps a job. We have not focused our attention on the health aspect of learning particularly at the basic level of brain function. A recent study supports the importance of stimulation seeking in 3 year-old children upon later development of intelligence, a clear environmental-neurophysiological relationship (Raine et al., 2002). Stimulation seeking may be taught to infants as one method to ignite the learning process similar to sign language discussed above.

The human brain is an information processor of unparallel proportion. There is a highly complex capacity of the human brain to process information simultaneously and in parallel fashion. The brain is capable of processing multiple stimuli from different modalities and derives meaning from each. That the brain processes information in such a complicated and unique manner is quite interesting. Beyond our typical approach of trying to understand how the brain processes information lays the critical question of why information processing occurs. Perhaps our brains require information inherently to develop and for health purposes. This argument suggests that the human brain requires stimulation and devoid of such will initiate self-stimulation. From this perspective, learning itself may be viewed as a health promoting behavior that is necessary for the human brain to thrive and develop. More significantly, with increased learning the human brain may develop in ways that promotes synaptic density and intellectual reserve. It is intellectual reserve that has been theorized to delay or perhaps even prevent neurodegenerative disease.

Learning as a health promoting behavior for brain wellness (Nussbaum, 2002) is a new concept deserving attention, particularly if a lifestyle for brain health is to be advanced. The process of learning must involve neurophysiological events that result in some morphological change of the brain. From the onset of stimulus perception to attention, encoding and eventual consolidation, information transforms the structure of our neuroanatomy and thought process. The frequency of learning yields many positive things that have been discussed in this book including intelligence, potential for advanced education, and potential for more sophisticated occupation. Each of these outcomes of learning is positive though they do not reflect the direct neurophysiological effect of a human brain undergoing the process of learning new information.

Learning is proposed as a direct health promoting behavior of the brain not unlike the benefit of running on a treadmill for the heart. This author advocates learning to be considered health promoting and to conceptualize learning as a type of "neuronal vaccine" that may provide some degree of insulation against neurodegeneration or brain insult. In a more modest manner, learning may delay clinical manifestation of neurodegenerative disease. Viewed from this perspective, health policy could champion lifelong learning and propose its inclusion in basic wellness programs offered by major health insurance carriers. While most of us attend learning programs for our employment or for obtaining credits we do not anticipate our learning to be health promoting. There is a need to define lifelong learning in a manner that permits such activity to demonstrate health-promoting benefit on a short term and longer-term basis. A major goal for the health of all Americans should be to support financially our continued learning as one means of promoting healthy brains across our lifespan.

Lifelong learning typically occurs in the form of workshops and training to be attended by those interested. College and universities represent a natural setting of formalized learning attended by more older adults than ever before. Less formal community-based learning occurs in senior centers and elder-hostel programs throughout the nation. However, we have not yet defined the concept of lifelong learning nor established standard methods to produce and market lifelong learning for health purposes. Measurement of lifelong learning on our health (preventative or delaying of disease contribution) is an empirical issue worthy of investigation, particularly with regards to the brain.

The type of subject matter when learning that provides the most value for brain health is not yet known. Soon, however, we may be able to understand the neuropsychological value of each activity based on how much brain stimulation is generated by engaging in the particular activity. Some activities will be idiosyncratic given the fact that everyone has a different history with different experiences. For example, some may benefit more from learning how to dance than those already exposed to such learning. In contrast, some activities may have a general value for all who choose to engage in them. One example might be reading and writing. Overall, my general advice to those who wish to know what they can do to promote the health of their brains is to engage in activities that are both *novel and complex*. It is the novel and complex activities that will challenge our brains and thereby promote brain health. The novel and complex activities are also the same activities that we find difficult, uncomfortable, and not much fun! Perhaps the motto of "no pain no gain" employed with physical exercise for cardiac health can also be applied for mental activities that promote brain health.

II.   Physical Activity

There is sufficient evidence to indicate that physical activity and exercise are health-promoting behaviors for the human being. Snowdon (2001) promotes walking as a primary behavior that can foster longevity. Physical exercise increases health for many different organ systems in the human and helps to limit risk of disease across the lifespan (Rowe & Kahn, 1998). Unfortunately, The MacArthur Foundation Study on Successful Aging (Rowe & Kahn) found that the average older person is not vigorously active and does not participate in regular walking let alone exercise. These authors estimated that nearly 33% of the women and 25% of men between the ages 65 and 74 reports no participation in leisure time physical activities such as tennis, golf, walking, or bicycling. For those over the age of 75 who represent an age cohort vulnerable to frailty, the numbers become even more troubling. Nearly half of the women and almost 40% of men over age 75 are considered sedentary and only 20% participate in some form of regular exercise.

There appears to be a natural tendency to become less active as we get older. This triggers a cascade of pathological events to include reduced energy, fatigue, muscle atrophy, malaise and reduced cardiac efficiency that can directly influence cognitive functioning. There is a constant risk of older persons falling prey to a self-fulfilling prophecy: "as I get older I am to be less active and to decline." It is important to note that our current social policy on retirement fosters such an attitude and belief system. Conceptually we do not view exercise as promoting brain health. Rather, we believe exercise is primarily for the health of the heart. Social change may include how the brain benefits from exercise and this could be articulated in every communication and recommendation on exercise provided by the government. Similarly, there may be utility in integrating cognitive exercise and brain health within the big business of aerobics and physical exercise.

Finally, while it is known that exercise has a tremendous benefit to physical, cognitive, and psychological health there has not been any formal integration of exercise into our health care system. Integration of the medical with the physical fitness business seems to make sense. Further, health insurance payers should incentivize financially membership within a supervised exercise program as part of every wellness program. Such payment for membership could be contingent on attendance at regular workouts as indicated by a doctor or coordinator managing the program. Payment for such ongoing physical exercise represents true proactive health care.

III.   Socialization and Involvement

Research has established the importance of an active and

social lifestyle for healthy brains (Bassuk et al., 1999; Fratiglioni et al., 2000; Friedland et al., 2001). Despite such research Americans tend not to remain active and many are drawn to sedentary and disengaged lifestyles. Many older Americans become isolated and passive in their daily course of events, a dangerous pathway to potential brain atrophy. Selection of our environments and the amount of socialization we maintain is critical for the health of our brains. A highly social individual is more likely to be exposed to novel and complex experiences. This may occur as a result of direct interaction with others or indirectly through the opportunities afforded by increased human interaction. Novelty and complexity represent the two critical factors for brain health proposed by this book. It is not coincidental that novelty and complexity are the opposite of passivity and rote. From a neurophysiological perspective it may be argued that more complex and novel tasks are those that demand greater utilization of our cortex relative to tasks that are passive and rote. For activities that are rote and passive we most likely rely upon our subcortical structures thought to be more involved in subconscious and procedural behaviors.

Travel is one social behavior identified as having a potentially positive effect on brain health by reducing the risk of dementia later in life (Fabrigoule et al., 1995). Travel is a good example of a behavior that is inherently novel and complex. With travel we expose our brains to new environments and it is the novelty of the new environment that can be complex. From a neurophysiological perspective, travel most likely places a relatively greater demand on our cortex compared to our subcortical structures. As our cortex is the highest order thinking part of our brain stimulation of this region can be argued to promote cortical growth via development of synaptic density. The learning that occurs in new environments lays down neuronal networks previously absent and helps to build up a type of defense against potential neurodegeneration. The direct relationship between environment and brain morphology must be recognized and employed to better foster activities that promote brain health.

The Problem with Retirement!

Retirement as it is presently conceptualized in our country rejects the importance of social interaction and engagement. We adopted a retirement age of 65 from Bismark who implemented similar policy in Germany 200 years ago! The entire concept of retirement runs counter to health promotion and certainly contradicts the belief that novelty and complexity promote brain health. According to the American Heritage Dictionary (1983) the word retirement means "to go away; depart, as for rest and seclusion; to withdraw from public life or active service." The studies by Friedland et al. (2001) and Bassuk et al. (1999) clearly demonstrate the negative impact on brain health (increased risk for dementia) when humans engage in predominantly passive activities and isolate from society.

This book has reviewed many animal studies that demonstrate brain atrophy with environments lacking enrichment. Human studies indicate social disengagement to increase cognitive decline in community dwelling older adults (Bassuk et al., 1999; Fratiglioni, et al., 2000). Retirement involves an almost natural increase in physical and mental isolation, neglect, and passivity. Conceptualized from a health promotion perspective, our national policy should encourage all functional members of society to remain as integrated and involved in meaningful activity for as long as possible. People should not be financially rewarded to segregate out of society.

While no one should be forced to keep working, no functional person should be forced or covertly encouraged to retire. Older persons can and should continue to work for as long as possible particularly if work provides a personally meaningful role and purpose. Without a role and purpose sickness and dependency can occur with increased utilization of the costly medical system. This author proposes functional status rather than chronological age as the determining factor regarding who works and who does not work. For those who cannot or choose not to work *a meaningful role and purpose is still needed*. Human beings require a purpose and meaning to our lives. Without such a meaning, role and purpose we will isolate and become ill. Clearly, active participation in society can be argued to be health promoting particularly since healthy individuals utilize the costly health care system less than those who are ill and probably less than those who perceive themselves ill because they are without purpose in their lives. A meaningful role and purpose may involve volunteer work and or an increase in daily physical activity. Those persons who have not planned for retirement either financially or by not developing lifespan hobbies are likely to end up isolated and passive. Success in late life is dependent upon success and planning in early life. To this end there is a real need for workshops and learning opportunities on successful aging across the lifespan.

Learning about successful aging must begin at the earliest ages. I have advocated coursework on how to age successfully within every grade school in our country. Such a policy shift is framed from a proactive health approach. Research suggests our children begin to learn what it means to be old by about age 8 and perhaps as early as age 4. The lessons of aging into late life tend not to be realistic and are certainly not positive. We have enough knowledge on how to age successfully across the lifespan to implement a standard course within our grade schools. Older adults could teach this course, as they are generally welcomed into classrooms by children. At present, there is very little discussion about aging in the latter lifespan in our schools, including medical schools, and if there is any coursework on aging it is typically a small part of a general health class. Imagine a standard course on how to age successfully across the lifespan with similar importance to English and Math. A primary reason for the course is the fact that many of our children today are going to live beyond eighty and ninety! It is critical to not only talk about the need to be active, but to educate at early ages how and why to be active. The consequences to health are significant and such early education on successful aging represents true proactive behavior.

Stick with the novel and complex!

References

Acredolo, L. P. & Goodwyn, S. W. (1985). Symbolic gesturing in language development. Human Development, 28, 40-49.

Acredolo, L. P. & Goodwyn, S. W. (1988). Symbolic gesturing in normal infants. Child Development, 59, 450-466.

Acredolo, L. P. & Goodwyn, S. W. (2000, July). The long-term impact of symbolic gesturing during infancy on I.Q. at age 8. Paper presented at the International Conference on Infant Studies, Brighton, UK.

Albert, M. S. (1995). How does education affect cognitive function? Annals of Epidemiology, 75, 76-78.

Albert, M. S. & Moss, M. B. (1988). Geriatric neuropsychology. New York: the Guilford Press.

Altman, J. (1962). Are new neurons formed in the brains of adult mammals? Science, 135, 1127-1128.

Altman, J. (1969). Autoradiographic and histological studies of postnatal neurogenesis IV. Cell proliferation and migration in the anterior forebrain, with special reference to persisting neurogenesis in the olfactory bulb. Journal of Comparative Neurology, 137, 433-458.

Altman, J. & Das, G. D. (1964). Autoradiographic examination of the effects of enriched environment on the rate of glial multiplication in the adult rat brain. Nature, 204, 1161-1163.

Altman, J. & Das, G. D. (1965). Autoradiographic and histologic evidence of postnatal hippocampal neurogenesis in rats. Journal of Comparative Neurology, 124, 319-335.

Angevine, J. B., & Cotman, C. W. (1981). Principles of neuroanatomy. New York: Oxford Press.

Arkin, S. M. (1999). Elder Rehab: A student-supervised exercise program for Alzheimer's patients. The Gerontologist, 39, 729-735.

Arkin, S. M. (2001). Alzheimer rehabilitation by students: Interventions and outcomes. Neuropsychological Rehabilitation, 11, 273-317.

Bartzokis, G., Beckson, M., Lu, P. H., Nuechterlein, H., Edwards, N., & Mintz, J. (2001). Age-related changes in frontal and temporal lobe volumes in men. General Psychiatry, 58, 461-465.

Bassuk, S. S., Glass, T. A., & Berkman, L. F. (1999). Social disengagement and incident cognitive decline in community-dwelling elderly persons. Annals of Internal Medicine, 131, 165-173.

Bayer, S., Yackel, J. W., & Puri, P. S. (1982). Neurons in the rat dentate gyrus granular layer substantially increase during juvenile and adult life. Science, 216, 890-892.

Beard, M. C., Kokmen, E., Offord, K. P., & Kurland, L. T. (1992). Lack of association between Alzheimer's disease and education, occupation, marital status, or living arrangement. Neurology, 42, 2063-2068.

Beaulieu, C., & Colonnier, M. (1987). Effect of the richness of the environment on the cat visual cortex. The Journal of Comparative Neurology, 266, 478-494.

Beck, H., Goussakov, I. V., Lie, A., Helmstaedter, C., & Elger, C. E. (2000). Synaptic plasticity in the human dentate gyrus. The Journal of Neuroscience, 20, 7080-7086.

Bellugi, U. (1994, August). Silence, signs, and wonder. Discover, 15, 60-68.

Bennett, E. L., Diamond, M. C., Krech, D., & Rosenzweig, M. R. (1964). Chemical and anatomical plasticity of brain. Science, 146, 610-619.

Berkman, L. F. (1986). The association between educational attainment and mental status examinations: of etiologic significance for senile dementias or not? Journal of Chronic Disease, 39, 171-174.

Bigler, E. D. (1997). Neuroimaging in normal aging and dementia. In P. D. Nussbaum (Ed.). Handbook of neuropsychology and aging (pp. 409-421). New York: Plenum Press.

Birse, S. C., Leonard, R. E., & Coggeshall, R. E. (1983). Comparative Neurology, 194, 291.

Bjornson, C. R. R., Rietze, R. L., Reynolds, B. A., Magli, C., & Vescovi, A. L. (1999). Turning brain into blood: A hematopoietic fate adopted by adult neural stem cells in vivo. Science, 283, 534-537.

Bowler, J. V., Munoz, D. G., Merskey, H., & Hachinski, V. (1998). Factors affecting the age of onset and rate of progression of Alzheimer's disease. Journal of Neurology, Neurosurgery, and Psychiatry, 65, 184-190.

Bryans, W. A. (1959). Mitotic activity in the brain of the adult white rat. Anatomical Record, 133, 65-71.

Chen, G., Rajkowska, G., Du, Fu., Seraji-Bozorgzad, N., & Manji, H. K. (2000). Enhancement of hippocampal neurogenesis by lithium. Journal of Neurochemistry, 75, 1729-1734.

Cobb, J. L., Wolf, P. A., White, R., & D'Agostino (1995). The effect of education on incidence of dementia and Alzheimer's disease in the Framingham study. Neurology, 45, 1707-1712.

Coffey, C. E., & Figiel, G. S. (1991). Neuropsychiatric significance of subcortical encephalomalacia. In B. J. Carroll & J. E. Barrett (Eds.). Psychopathology and the brain (pp. 243-264). New York: Raven Press.

Coffey, C. E., Lucke, J. F., Saxton, J. A., Ratcliff, G., Unitas, L. J., Billig, B., Bryan, R. N. (1998). Sex differences in brain aging: a quantitative magnetic resonance imaging study. Archives of Neurology, 55, 169-179.

Cohen, G. D. (2001). The Creative Age. New York: Quill.

Collins, P. (2001). Language: The hands that hold the keys. Nature Reviews Neuroscience, 2, 76.

Cooper, K. H. (1994). The antioxidant revolution. Nashville: Nelson Publishers.

Corder, R., Douthwaite, J. A., Lees, D. M., Khan, N. Q., Santos, A. C., Wood, E. G., & Carrier, M. J. (2001). Health: Endothelin-1 synthesis reduced by red wine. Nature, 414, 863-964.

Cotman, C. W. & Berchtold, N. C. (2002). Exercise: a behavioral intervention to enhance brain health and plasticity. Trends in Neurosciences, 25, 6.

Cotman, C. W., & Engesser-Cesar, C. (2002). Exercise enhances and protects brain function. Exercise and Sports Science Reviews, 30, 75-79.

Crair, M. C. (1999). Neuronal activity during development: permissive or instructive? Current Opinion in Neurobiology, 9, 88-93.

Dash, P. K., Mach, S. A., & Moore, A. N. (2001). Enhanced neurogenesis in the rodent hippocampus following traumatic brain injury. Journal of Neuroscience Research, 63, 313-319.

Dekaban, A. S., & Sadowsky, B. S. (1978). Changes in brain weights during the span of human life: Relation of brain weights to body height and weight. Annals of Neurology, 4, 345-357.

Diamond, M. C., & Hopson, J. (1998). Magic trees of the mind. New York: Plume.

Diamond, M. C., Ingham, C. A., Johnson, R. E., Bennett, E. L., & Rosenzweig, M. R. (1978). Effects of environment on morphology of rat cerebral cortex and hippocampus. Journal of Neurobiology, 7, 75-85.

Diamond, M. C., Krech, D., Rosenzweig, M. R. (1964). The effects of an enriched environment on the histology of the rat cerebral cortex. Journal of Comparative Neurology, 123, 111-120.

Eckenhoff, M. F., & Rakic, P. (1988). Nature and fate of proliferative cells in the hippocampal dentate gyrus during the lifespan of the rhesus monkey. Journal of Neuroscience, 8, 2729-2747.

Eriksson, P. S., Perfilieva, E., Bjork-Eriksson, T., Alborn, A. M., Nordborg, C., Peterson, D. A., & Gage, F. H. (1998). Neurogenesis in the adult human hippocampus. Nature Medicine, 4, 1313-1317.

Evans, D. A., Hebert, L. E., Beckett, L. A., Scherr, P. A., Albert, M. S., Chown, M. J., Pilgrim, D. M., Taylor, J. O. (1997). Education and other measures of socioeconomic status and risk of incident Alzheimer Disease in a defined population of older persons. Archives of Neurology, 54, 1399-1405.

Faber, V. M., Bootsma-Wiel, A., Exel, E. V., Gussekloo, J., Lagaay, A. M., Dongen, E. V., Knook, D. L., Geest, S. V. D., Westendorp, R., G., J. (2001). Successful aging in the oldest old. Archives of Internal Medicine, 161, 2694-2700.

Fabrigoule, C., Letenneur, L., Dartigues, F. J., Zarrouk, M., Commenges, D., & Gateau, B., P. (1995). Social and leisure activities and risk of dementia: A prospective longitudinal study. Journal of the American Geriatrics Society, 43, 485-490.

Francis, D. D., & Meaney, M. J. (1999). Maternal care and the development of stress responses. Current Opinion in Neurobiology, 9, 128-134.

Fratiglioni, L., Wang, H-X, Ericsson, K., Maytan, M., & Winblad, B. (2000). Influence of social network on occurrence of dementia: a community-based longitudinal study. Lancet, 355, 1315-1319.

Friedland, R. P., Fritsch, T., Smyth, K. A., Koss, E., Lerner, A. J., Chen, C. H., Petot, G. J., & Debanne, S. M. (2001). Patients with Alzheimer's disease have reduced activities in midlife compared with healthy control-group members. Procedings of the National Academy of Sciences, 98, 3440-3445.

Giedd, J. N., Blumenthal, J., Jeffries, N. O., Castellanos, F. X., Liu, H., Zijdenbos, A., Paus, T., Evans, A. C., & Rapoport, J. L. (1999). Brain development during childhood and adolescence: a longitudinal MRI study. Nature Neuroscience, 2, 861-863.

Goldman, S. A., & Nottenbohm, F. (1983). Neuronal production, migration, and differentiation in a vocal control nucleus of the adult female canary brain. Proceedings of the National Academy of Sciences, 80, 2390-2394.

Goodwyn, S. W., Acredolo, L. P., & Brown, C. A. (2000). Impact of symbolic gesturing on early language development. Journal of Nonverbal Behavior, 24, 81-103.

Gould, E., Beylin, A., Tanapat, P., Reeves, A., & Shors, T. J. (1999A). Learning enhances adult neurogenesis in the hippocampal formation. Nature Neuroscience, 2, 260-265.

Gould, E., & Gross, C. G. (2000). New neurons: Extraordinary evidence or extraordinary conclusion? Science, 288, 771A.

Gould, E., Reeves, A. J., Fallah, M., Tanapat, P., Gross, C. G., & Fuchs, E. (1999B). Hippocampal neurogenesis in adult old world primates. Proceedings of the National Academy of Sciences, 96, 5263-5267.

Gould, E., Reeves, A. J., Graziano, M. S. A., & Gross, C. G. (1999C). Neurogenesis in the neocortex of adult primates. Science, 286, 548-552.

Gould, E., & Tanapat, P. (1999). Stress and hippocampal neurogenesis. Society of biological psychiatry, 46, 1472-1479.

Gould, E., Tanapat, P., Hastings, N. B., & Shors, T. J. (1999D). Neurogenesis in adulthood: a possible role in learning. Trends in Cognitive Science, 3, 186-192.

Greenough, W., Cohen, N. J., & Juraska, J. M. (1999). New neurons in old brains: learning to survive. Nature Neuroscience, 2, 203-205.

Gronbaek, M., Becker, U., Johansen, D., Gottschau, A., Schnohr, P., Hein, H. O., Jensen, G., & Sorensen, T. (2000). The relationship between type of alcoholic drinks consumed and death from various causes. Annals of Internal Medicine, 133, 1-22.

Gross, C. G. (2000). Neurogenesis in the adult brain: death of a dogma. Nature Reviews Neuroscience, 1, 67-73.

Gurland, B. J. (1981). The borderlands of dementia: the influence of socioecultural characteristics on rates of dementia occurring in the senium. Aging, 15, 61-84.

Hamilton, A. (1901). The division of differentiated cells in the central nervous system of the white rat. Journal of Comparative Neurology, 11, 297-320.

Horn, J. L., & Catell, R. B. (1967). Age differences in fluid and crystallized intelligence. Acta Psychobiologica, 26, 107-129.

Jacobson, M. (1970). Developmental neurobiology. New York: Holt, Rinehart, and Winston.

Johansson, C. B., Momma, S., Clarke, D. L., Risling, M., Lendahl, U., & Frisen, J. (1999). Identification of a neural stem cell in the adult mammalian central nervous system. Cell, 96, 25-34.

Jorm, A. F. (1997). Alzheimer's disease: risk and protection. Medical Journal of the Aged, 167, 443-446.

Jorm, A. F., Rodgers, B., Henderson, A. S., Korten, A. E., Jacomb, P. A., Christensen, H., & Mackinnon, A. (1998). Occupation type as a predictor of cognitive decline and dementia in old age. Age and Ageing, 27, 477-483.

Kaplan, M. S. (1981). Neurogenesis in the 3-month-old rat visual cortex. Journal of Comparative Neurology, 195, 323-338.

Kaplan, M. S. (1984). Mitotic neuroblasts in the 9 day old and 11-month old rodent hippocampus. Journal of Neuroscience, 4, 1429-1441.

Kaplan, M. S. (1985). Formation and turnover of neurons in young and senescent animals: an electron microscopic and morphometric analysis. Annals of New York Academy of Science, 457, 173-192.

Kaplan, M. S., & Hinds, J. W. (1977). Neurogenesis in the adult rat: electron microscopic analysis of light radioautographs. Science, 197, 1092-1094.

Katzman, R (1993). Education and the prevalence of dementia and Alzheimer's disease. Neurology, 43, 13-20.

Katzman, R. (1995). Can late life social or leisure activities delay the onset of dementia? Journal of the American Geriatrics Society, 43, 583-584.

Kempermann, G. (2002). Why new neurons? Possible function for adult hippocampal neurogenesis. Journal of Neurosciences, 22, 635-638.

Kempermann, G., Brandon, E. P., & Gage, F. H. (1998). Environmental stimulation of 129/SvJ mice causes increased cell proliferation and neurogenesis in the adult dentate gyrus. Current Biology, 8, 939-942.

Kempermann, G., & Gage, F. H. (1998). Closer to neurogenesis in adult humans. Nature Medicine, 4, 555-557.

Kempermann, G., & Gage, F. H. (1999). Experience-dependent regulation of adult hippocampal neurogenesis: Effects of long-term stimulation and stimulus withdrawal (1999). Hippocampus, 9, 321-332.

Kempermann, G., Kuhn, H. G., & Gage, F. H. (1997). More hippocampal neurons in adult mice living in an enriched environment. Nature, 386, 493-495.

Kempermann, G., Kuhn, H. G., & Gage, F. H. (1998). Experience-induced neurogenesis in the senescent dentate gyrus. The Journal of Neuroscience, 18, 3206-3212.

Koenig, H. G. (1995). Religion and health in later life. In M. Kimble, S. Mcfadden, J. Ellor, & J. Seeber (Eds.). Aging, spirituality, and religion. Minneapolis: Fortress Press.

Kolb, B., & Wishaw, I. Q. (1990). Fundamentals of human neuropsychology (3rd edition.). New York: W. H. Freeman and Company.

Kolb, B., & Wishaw, I. Q. (1998). Brain plasticity and behavior. Annual Reviews of Psychology, 49, 43-64.

Kotulak, R. (1997). Inside the brain: Revolutionary discoveries of how the mind works. Kansas City, MO: Anreas and McMeely.

Kornak, D. R., & Rakic, P. (1999A). Continuation of neurogenesis in the hippocampus of the adult macaque monkey. Proceedings of the National Academy of Science, 457, 143-161.

Kornak, D. R., & Rakic, P. (1999B). Cell proliferation without neurogenesis in adult primate neocortex. Science, 294, 2127-2130.

La Rue, A. (1992). Aging and neuropsychological assessment. New York: Plenum Press.

Lee, C. K., Klopp, R. G., Weindruch, R., & Prolla, T. A. (1999). Gene expression profile of aging and its retardation by caloric restriction. Science, 285, 1390-1393.

Leibovici, D., Ritchie, K., Ledesert, B., & Touchon, J. (1998). Age and Ageing, 25, 392-397.

Lemaire, V., Koehl, M., Moal, M. L., & Abrous, D. N. (2000). Prenatal stress produces learning deficits associated with an inhibition of neurogenesis in the hippocampus. Proceedings of the National Academy of Sciences, 97, 11032-11037.

Lewis, S. C., Dennis, M. S., O'Rourke, S. J., & Sharpe, M. (2001). Negative attitudes among short-term stroke survivors predict worse long-term survival. Stroke, 32, 1640-1647.

Liu, Solway, K., Messing, R. O., & Sharp, F. R. (1998). Increased neurogenesis in the dentate gyrus after transient global ischemia in gerbils. The Journal of Neuroscience, 18, 7768-7778.

Madsen, T. M., Bengzon, T. A., Bolwig, T. G., Lindvall, O., & Tingstrm, A. (2000). Increased neurogenesis in a model of electroconvulsive therapy. Biological Psychiatry, 47, 1043-1049.

Malberg, J. E., Eisch, A. J., Nestler, E. J., & Duman, R. S. (2000). Chronic antidepressant treatment increases neurogenesis in adult rat hippocampus. The Journal of Neuroscience, 20, 9104-9110.

McEwen, B. S. (1999). Stress and hippocampal plasticity. Annual Review of Neuroscience, 22, 105-122.

Meaney, M. J., Aitken, D. H., V. Berkel, C., Bhatnagar, S., & Sapolsky, R. M. (1998). Science, 239, 766-768.

Moceri, V. M., Kukull, W. A., Emanuel, I., Van Belle, G., & Larson, E. B. (2000). Early-life risk factors and the development of Alzheimer's disease. Neurology, 54, 415-420.

Mortensen, E. L., Michaelsen, K. F., Sanders, S. A., & Reinisch, J. M. (2002). The association between duration of breastfeeding and adult intelligence. Journal of the American Medical Association, 287, 2365-2371.

Mortimer, J. A. (1997). Brain reserve and the clinical expression of Alzheimer's disease. Geriatrics, 52, S50-S53.

Nakamura, H., Kobayashi, S., Ohashi, Y. (1999). Age-changes of brain synapses and synaptic plasticity in response to an enriched environment. Journal of Neuroscience Research, 56, 307-315.

Nathanielsz, P. W. (1999). Life in the womb: The origin of health and disease. New York: Promothean Press.

Nilsson, M., Perfilieva, E., Johansson, U., Orwar, O., & Eriksson, P. S. (1999). Enriched environment increases neurogenesis in the adult rat dentate gyrus and improves spatial memory. Journal of Neurobiology, 39, 569-578.

Nottenbohm, F. (1985). Neuronal replacement in adulthood. Annals of New York Academy of Science, 457, 143-161.

Nottenbohm, F. (1996). The King Solomon lectures in neuroethology. A white canary on Mount Acropolis. Journal of Comparative Physiology, 179, 149-156.

Nowakowski, R. S., & Hayes, N. L. (2000). New neurons: Extraordinary evidence or extraordinary conclusion? Science, 288, 771A.

Null, G. (2000). The food-mood-body connection. New York: Seven Stories Press.

Nussbaum, P. D. (1998). Neuropsychological assessment of the elderly. In G. Goldstein, P. D. Nussbaum, & S. R. Beers (Eds.). Neuropsychology (pp. 83-101). New York: Plenum Press.

Nussbaum, P.D. (2002). Learning: Towards health and the human condition. Educational Technology, 42, 35-39.

Oitzl, M. S., Workel, J. O., Fluttert, M., Frosch, F., & Kloet, R. d. (2000). Maternal deprivation affects behavior from youth to senescence: amplification of individual differences in spatial learning and memory in senescent Brown Norway rats. European Journal of Neuroscience, 12, 3771-3780.

Orgogozo, J. M., Dartigues, J. F., Lafont, S., Letenneur, L., Commenges, D., Salaon, R., Renaud, S., & Breteler, M. B. (1997). Wine consumption and dementia in the elderly: a prospective community study in the Bordeaux area. Reviews in Neurology, 153, 185-192.

Ornish, D. (1990). Reversing heart disease. New York: Random House.

Patton, J. A., & Nottenbohm, F. N. (1984). Neurons generated in the adult brain are recruited into functional circuits. Science, 225, 1046-1048.

Petito, L. A., Holowka, S., H., Sergio, L. E., & Ostry, D. (2001). Language rhythms in baby-hand movements. Nature, 413, 35-36.

Petitto, L. A., Zattore, R. J., Guana, K., Nikelski, E. J., Dostie, D., & Evans, A. C. (2000). Speech-like cerebral activity in profoundly deaf people while processing signed languages: Implications for the neural basis of all human language. Proceedings of the National Academy of Sciences, 97, 13961-13966.

Pfeffer, R. I., Afifi, A. A., Chance, J. M. (1987). Prevalence of Alzheimer's disease in a retirement community. American Journal of Epidemiology, 125, 420-436.

Plassman, B. L., Havlik, R. J., Steffens, D. C., Helms, M. J., Newman, T. N., Drosdick, D., Phillips, C., Gau, B. A., Welsh-Bohmer, K. A., Burke, J. R., Guralnik, J. & M., Breitner, J. C. S. (2000). Documented head injury in early adulthood and risk of Alzheimer's disease and other dementias. Neurology, 55, 1158-1166.

Plassman, B. L., Welsh, K. A., Helms, M., Brandt, J., Page, W. F., & Breitner, J. C. S. (1995). Intelligence and education as predictors of cognitive state in late life: A 50-year follow-up. Neurology, 45, 1446-1450.

Powers, R. E. (1994). Neurobiology of aging. In C. E. Coffey & J. L. Cummings (Eds.). Textbook of geriatric neuropsychiatry (pp. 35-70). Washington DC: American Psychiatric Press.

Pruessner, J. C., Collins, D. L., Pruessner, M., & Evans, A. C. (2001). Age and gender predict volume decline in the anterior and posterior hippocampus in early adulthood. The Journal of Neuroscience, 21, 194-200.

Rakic, P. (1985). Limits of neurogenesis in primates. Science, 227, 1054-1056.

Rakic, P. (2002). Neurogenesis in the adult primate neocortex: an evaluation of the evidence. Nature Reviews Neuroscience, 3, 65-71.

Ramon, Y., & Cajal. (1928). Degeneration and regeneration of the nervous system. (translated from the 1913 Spanish Edition) London: Oxford University Press.

Raine, A., Reynolds, C., Venables, P. H., & Mednick, S. A. (2002). Stimulation seeking and intelligence: A prospective longitudinal study. Journal of Personality and Social Psychology, 82, 663-674.

Reiman, E. M., Caselli, R. J., Yun, L. S., Chen, K., Bandy, D., Minoshima, S., Thibodeau, S. N., & Osborne, D. (1996). Preclinical evidence of Alzheimer's disease in persons homozygous for the E4 allele for apolipoprotein E. The New England Journal of Medicine, 334, 752-758.

Reiman, E. M., Uecker, A., Caselli, R. J., Lewis, S., Brandy, D., De Leon, M. J., De Santi, S., Convit, A., Osborne, D., Weaver, A., & Thibodeau, S. N. (1998). Hippocampal volumes in cognitively normal persons at risk for Alzheimer's disease. Annals of Neurology, 44, 288-291.

Reynolds, B. A., & Weiss, S. (1992). Generation of neurons and astrocytes from isolated cells of the adult mammalian nervous system. Science, 255, 1707-1710.

Reynolds, B. A., & Weiss, S. (1996). Clonal and population analyses demonstrate that an EGF-responsive mammalian embryonic precursor is a stem cell. Developmental Biology, 175, 1-13.

Richards, M. (2000). Cognitive links across the lifecourse and implications for health in later life. Age and Ageing, 29, 477-478.

Rosenzweig, M. R., & Bennett, E. L. (1996). Psychobiology of plasticity: effects of training and experience on brain and behavior. Behavioural Brain Research, 78, 57-65.

Rosenzweig, M. R., Bennett, E. L., Hebert, M., & Morimoto, H. (1978). Social grouping cannot account for cerebral effects of enriched environments. Brain Research, 153, 563-576.

Rosenzweig, M. R., Krech, D., Bennett, E. L., & Diamond, M. C. (1962). Effects of environmental complexity and training on the brain chemistry and anatomy: A replication and extension. Journal of Comparative Physiology and Psychology, 55, 429-437.

Rowe, J. W., & Kahn, R. L. (1998). Successful aging. New York: Pantheon Books.

Roy, N. S., Wang, S., Jiang, L., Kang, J., Benraiss, A., Restelli, C. H., Fraser, R. A. R., Couldwell, W. T., Kawaguchi, A., Okano, H., Nedergaard, M., & Goldman, S. A. (2000). In vitro neurogenesis by progenitor cells isolated from the adult human hippocampus. Nature Medicine, 6, 271-277.

Salat, D. H., Kaye, J. A., & Janowsky, J. S. (1999). Prefrontal gray and white matter volumes in healthy aging and Alzheimer's disease. Archives of Neurology, 56, 338-344.

Salmon, D., & Bondi, M. (1997). Alzheimer's Disease. In Nussbaum, P.D. (Ed.), Handbook of neuropsychology and Aging (pp. 141-158). New York: Plenum Publishing.

Sanjay, M. S., Leavitt, B. R., & Jeffrey, M. D. (2000). Induction of neurogenesis in the neocortex of adult mice. Nature, 405, 951-955.

Sapolsky, R. M. (1996). Why stress is bad for your brain. Science, 273, 749-750.

Sapolsky, R. M. (1998). Why elephants don't get ulcers. New York: W. H. Freeman.

Schaie, K. W. (1990). Intellectual development in adulthood. In J. E. Birren, & K. Warner Schaie (Eds.), Handbook of psychology of aging (pp. 291-304). San Diego: Academic Press.

Schmand, B., Smit, J. H., Geerlings, M. I., & Lindeboom, J. (1997). The effects of intelligence and education on the development of dementia. A test of the brain reserve hypothesis. Psychological Medicine, 27, 1337-1344.

Schmand, B., Smit, J., Lindeboom, J., Smits, C., Hooijer, C., Jonker, C., & Deelman, B. (1997). Low education is a genuine risk factor for accelerated memory decline and dementia. Journal of Clinical Epidemiology, 50, 1025-1033.

Sharp, P. E., McNaughton, B. L., & Barnes, C. A. (1985). Enhancement of hippocampal field potentials in rats exposed to a novel, complex environment. Brain Research, 339, 361-365.

Shen, J., Barnes, C. A., McNaughton, B. L., Skaggs, W. E., & Weaver, K. L. (1997). The effects of aging on experience-dependent plasticity in hippocampal place cells. The Journal of Neuroscience, 17, 6769-6782.

Smart, I. (1961). The subependymal layer of the mouse brain and its cell production as shown by autography after H30 thymidine injection. Journal of Comparative Neurology, 116, 325-347.

Smith, M. A. (1996). Hippocampal vulnerability to stress and aging: possible role of neurotrophic factors. Behavioral Brain Research, 78, 25-36.

Snowdon, D. A. (2001). Aging with Grace. New York: Bantam Books.

Snowdon, D. A., Kemper, S. J., Mortimer, J. A., Greiner, L. H., Wekstein, D. R., & Markesbery, W. R. (1996). Linguistic ability in early life and cognitive function and Alzheimer's disease in late life: Findings from the Nun Study. Journal of the American Medical Association, 275, 528-532.

Soffie, M., Hahn, K., Terao, E., & Eclancher, F. (1999). Behavioural and glial changes in old rats following environmental enrichment. Behavioural Brain Research, 101, 37-49.

Sowell, E. R., Thompson, P. M., Holmes, C. J., Jernigan, T. L., & Toga, A. W. (1999). In vivo evidence for post-adolescent brain maturation in frontal and striatal regions. Nature Neuroscience, 2, 859- 861.

Spatz, H., C., (1996). Hebb's concept of synaptic plasticity and neuronal cell assemblies. Behavioral Brain Research, 78, 3-7.

Squire, L. (1987). Memory and brain. New York: Oxford Press.

Starr, J. M., Deary, I. J., Lemmon, H., & Whalley, L. J. (2000). Mental ability age 11 years and health status age 77 years. Age and Ageing, 29, 523-528.

Starratt, C., & Peterson, L. (1998). Personality and normal aging. In P.D. Nussbaum (Ed.). Handbook of neuropsychology and aging (pp. 15-31). New York: Plenum Press.

Stern, Y., Alexander, G. E., Prohovnik, I., & Mayeux, R. (1992). Inverse relationship between education and parietotemporal perfusion deficit in Alzheimer's disease. Annals of Neurology, 32, 371-375.

Stern, Y., Alexander, G. E., Prohovnik, I., Stricks, L., Link, B., Lennon, M. C., & Mayeux, R. (1995). Relationship between lifetime occupation and parietal flow. Neurology, 45, 55-60.

Stern, Y., Gurland, B., Tatemichi, T. K., Tang, M. X., Wilder, D., & Mayeux, R. (1994). Influence of education and occupation on the incidence of Alzheimer's disease. Journal of the American Medical Association, 271, 1004-1010.

Stern, Y., Tang, M. X., Denaro, J., & Mayeux, R. (1995). Increased risk of mortality in Alzheimer's disease patients with more advanced educational and occupational attainment. Annals of Neurology, 37, 590-595.

The American Heritage Dictionary (1983). New York: Dell Publishing.

Thompson, R. A., & Nelson, C. A. (2001). Developmental science and the media. <u>American Psychologist,</u> <u>56</u>, 5-15.

Torres-Gil, F. M. (1992). <u>The new aging</u>. West Port: Auburn House.

United States Census Bureau (2001). <u>Resident population estimates of the United States by age and sex: April 1, 1990 to July 1, 1999, with short-term projection to November 1, 2000.</u> Population estimates program, Washington, D.C: US Census Bureau.

Van Praag, Christie, B. R., Sejnowski, T. J., & Gage, F. H. (1999). Running enhances neurogenesis, learning, and long-term potentiation in mice. <u>Proceedings of the National Academy of Sciences of the United States of America, 96</u>, 13427-13431.

Van Praag, H., Kempermann, G., & Gage, F. H. (1999). Running increases cell proliferation and neurogenesis in the adult mouse dentate gyrus. <u>Nature Neuroscience, 2</u>, 266-270.

Van Praag, H., Kempermann, G., & Gage, F. H. (2000). Neural consequences of environmental enrichment. <u>Nature Reviews Neuroscience, 1</u>, 191-198.

Verghese, J., Lipton, R.B., Katz, M.J., Hall, C.B., Derby, C.A., Kuslansky, G., Ambrose, A.F., Sliwinksi, W., Buschke, H. (2003). Leisure activities and the risk of dementia in the elderly. <u>The New England Journal of Medicine, 348, 2508-2516.</u>

Walsh, R. N. & Cummins, R. A. (1975). Mechanisms mediating the production of environmentally induced brain changes. <u>Psychological Bulletin, 82</u>, 986-1000.

Walsh, R. N., & Cummins, R. A. (1979). Changes in hippocampal neuronal nuclei in response to environmental stimulation. International Journal of Neuroscience, 9, 209-212.

Wechsler, D. (1958). The measurement and appraisal of adult intelligence (4th ed.). Baltimore: Williams and Wilkins.

Welch, B. L., Brown, D. G., Welch, A. S., & Lin, D. C. (1974). Isolation, restrictive confinement or crowding of rats for one year. 1. Weight, nucleic acids and protein of brain regions. Brain Research, 75, 71-84.

Whalley, L. J., Starr, J. M., Athawes, R., Hunter, D., Pattie, A., & Deary, I. J. (2000). Childhood mental ability and dementia. Neurology, 55, 1455-1459.

Whalley, (2001). The Aging Brain. New York: Columbia University Press.

Wilson, R. S., Bennett, D. A., & Swartzendruber, A. (1998). Age-related change in cognitive function. In P. D. Nussbaum (Ed.). Handbook of neuropsychology and aging (pp. 7-14). New York: Plenum Press.

Wilson, R. S., Leon, Mendes De Leon, C. F., Barnes, L. L., Schneider, J. A., Bienias, J. L., Evans, D. A., & Bennett, D. A. (2002). Participation in cognitively stimulating activities and risk of incident Alzheimer's disease. Journal of the American Medical Association, 287, 742-748.

Lifestyle for a
Healthy Brain

1. **Do Not Smoke**

2. **Maintain Regular Physical Exams and Follow Your Physician's Advice**

3. **Learn New Information and Engage in the Complex and Novel**

4. **Engage in Regular Exercise to Include Daily Walking**

5. **Socialize, Have Fun, and Slow Down**

6. **Be Financially Stable and Hire a Financial Planner**

7. **Be Spiritual and Engage in Daily Prayer or Meditation**

8. **Eat Less and Include Antioxidants**

9. **Maintain Strong Family and Friendship Networks**

10. **Do Not Retire and Maintain a Role and Purpose**